Cathi Weber

S0-AIC-406

Dangerous
Wonder

Dangerous Wonder

the adventure of childlike faith

MICHAEL YACONELLI

NAVPRESS

BRINGING TRUTH TO LIFE

NavPress Publishing Group

P.O. Box 35001, Colorado Springs, Colorado 80935

The Navigators is an international Christian organization. Our mission is to reach, disciple, and equip people to know Christ and to make Him known through successive generations. We envision multitudes of diverse people in the United States and every other nation who have a passionate love for Christ, live a lifestyle of sharing Christ's love, and multiply spiritual laborers among those without Christ.

NavPress is the publishing ministry of The Navigators. NavPress publications help believers learn biblical truth and apply what they learn to their lives and ministries. Our mission is to stimulate spiritual formation among our readers.

© 1998 by Michael Yaconelli
All rights reserved. No part of this publication may be reproduced in any form without written permission from NavPress, P.O. Box 35001, Colorado Springs, CO 80935.
Library of Congress Catalog Card Number: 98-11297
ISBN 1-57683-046-2

Photo by Superstock

Some of the anecdotal illustrations in this book are true to life and are included with the permission of the persons involved. All other illustrations are composites of real situations, and any resemblance to people living or dead is coincidental.

Unless otherwise identified, all Scripture quotations in this publication are taken from the HOLY BIBLE: NEW INTERNATIONAL VERSION ® (NIV®). Copyright © 1973, 1978, 1984 by International Bible Society. Used by permission of Zondervan Publishing House. All rights reserved. Other versions used include: The Message: New Testament with Psalms and Proverbs (MSG) by Eugene H. Peterson, copyright © 1993, 1994, 1995, used by permission of NavPress Publishing Group; the New Revised Standard Version (NRSV), copyright 1989, by the Division of Christian Education of the National Council of the Churches of Christ in the USA, used by permission, all rights reserved; The Living Bible (TLB), copyright © 1971, used by permission of Tyndale House Publishers, Inc., Wheaton, IL 60189, all rights reserved; The New Jerusalem Bible (NJB), copyright © 1985 by Darton, Longman & Todd, Ltd., and Doubleday & Company, Inc., the New American Standard Bible (NASB), © The Lockman Foundation 1960, 1962, 1963, 1968, 1971, 1972, 1973, 1975, 1977; and the King James Version (KJV).

Printed in the United States of America

Yaconelli, Mike
     Dangerous wonder : the adventure of childlike faith / Michael Yaconelli.
        p.   cm.
     ISBN 1-57683-046-2
     1. Faith. I. Title.
  BV4637.Y33 1998
  234'.23—dc21   98-11297
                                            CIP

1 2 3 4 5 6 7 8 9 10 11 12 13 14 15/05 04 03 02 01 00 99 98

FOR A FREE CATALOG OF
NAVPRESS BOOKS & BIBLE STUDIES,
CALL 1-800-366-7788 (USA)
OR 1-416-499-4615 (CANADA)

Published in association with the literary agency of
Wolgemuth & Hyatt , Inc., Brentwood, Tennessee

To my wife, Karla,
who loved me into the presence of
the dangerous Jesus,
living just beyond my wildest dreams.

Contents

Acknowledgments

SPECIAL ACKNOWLEDGMENT

In the summer of 1994, thirteen men came together at a retreat center on the Gulf of Mexico. The weather was typical for that time of year: hot and muggy. We had come together at the invitation of a mutual friend to see if a group of strangers from a wide diversity of backgrounds could find community in our common faith in Jesus Christ. It is difficult for men to be with other men they don't know. Male bonding is not always what it's cracked up to be, and we found ourselves afraid, awkward, insecure, and clumsy in our meetings together.

One participant remained in the background. His silence was not a shy silence; it was careful and keenly observant. He didn't say much. He listened. He made us all a little nervous because it was obvious he was listening to our souls, not just our words.

One night, late, with the smothering humidity making sleep impossible, I decided to walk on the beach in front of our retreat center. I bumped into this man who had been silent. As I passed by, he looked up and said, "I think we could be friends." It was one of the few times in my life I had nothing to say. Caught completely off guard, I stood for a moment taking in his words. He had spoken with authority, and I realized he was right.

His name was Devlin Donaldson.

Devlin is a big man—and when you combine his size with a ponytail and a scraggly beard, he can be intimidating. We sat on an old fishing pier and talked for hours. I expected loud . . . what I got was gentle. I expected confidence and swagger,

9

what I discovered was humility and brokenness. Working for Compassion International, Devlin has spent most of his life connecting poor children from all over the world with American sponsors, and, as a result, he has been "ruined" by Jesus.

I like people who have been ruined by Jesus. Their souls have been permanently scarred by God's love. I like Devlin Donaldson. And lest you get the wrong impression, Devlin knows how to listen and how to dance. He is not just gentle, loving, and compassionate, he is also wild, crazy, and incredibly creative.

"Let's write a book about childlike faith," he blurted out one night.

"Yeah, right," I said. "All we have to do is get a publisher, and, the last time I checked, you don't just walk in and get a book contract."

"No problem," he said. "I'll get the contract." Two years later he called me to say we had a contract for a book on childlike faith.

Now we had a contract and no book.

We were going to write the book together, but, because of a number of logistical difficulties, I ended up writing the book. But Devlin Donaldson made it happen. Intuitively, Devlin found a way to connect my oddball view of the gospel with an idea that made sense—childlike faith. Were it not for the constant encouragement and humility of Devlin Donaldson, I would never have written this book.

OTHER ACKNOWLEDGMENTS

To Liz Heaney, my tough-as-nails editor, who has earned the affectionate monicker "hatchet lady" in the world of editing. She was not a "hatchet lady" with me. I watched her operate like an experienced surgeon with the manuscript, carefully and methodically using her scalpel with skill and care. Yet she has been more than a surgeon; she has been counselor, mother, friend, parent, pastor, and encourager.

Acknowledgments

How an editor works with an author like me is a mystery. During the writing of this book, I have managed to be a demanding, procrastinating, egocentric, insecure, emotionally unstable, fragile prima donna—stubborn and resistant one minute, weak and indecisive the next. Navigating Mike Yaconelli is not easy, but Liz found a way to accomplish it with dignity and sensitivity. Writing a book must be like delivering a child (except it takes longer), and, if I am correct, Liz has been one heck of a midwife. She has been thoroughly professional, precise, direct, fair, and most of all, passionate about the gospel. It has been an honor to work with her.

There are many others I should thank: My family for putting up with me during the long hours I ignored them while staring at a blank page. Danna Ayers, my assistant, who has strategically negotiated my paper-strewn office, cluttered desk, and periodic grumpiness when words were not coming. I deeply appreciate Glenn and Mildred Warner, whose hospitality allowed me to write at their beautiful home on the Klamath River. I am indebted to the warm and irregular congregation of Grace Community Church, from whom most of my understanding of the gospel comes. I cannot forget all of my employees at Youth Specialties, who allowed me a sabbatical so I could finish this book.

The late Henri Nouwen, Sue Mosteller, and the entire L'Arche community in Toronto, Canada, who started me on this wild and terrifying journey with Jesus in the first place, have my undying gratitude.

Lastly, my father, whose honesty and commitment to Christ have mentored me the fifty-five years of my life, and my mother and grandmother, both writers, who immersed my childhood with a love of words and a longing for Jesus, have my deep admiration and love.

Introduction

THE PLACE ALL CHILDREN KNOW ABOUT

When I was six years old, my favorite comic book character was Superman. I admired his strength, his x-ray vision, his colorful uniform and bright red cape. What captured my imagination most was Superman's ability to fly. Many of my childhood fantasies were about flying. I wanted to fly! I honestly believed flying was still a possibility. I would talk my friends into playing Superman, and they would play for a while, but soon they would tire of the game because I wouldn't let anyone else be Superman. I *had* to be Superman, I told them, because I knew more about flying than they did.

Sneaking into my parents' bathroom, I would find the stash of forbidden towels (the thick, new ones reserved only for guests). Once outside, with the towel tied around my neck and dragging on the dirt behind me, I would run as fast as I could and jump off the highest survivable launching pad I could find. With arms outstretched, cape billowing behind me, wind rushing past my ears, I believed I was flying.

Then came a day when, without warning, without provocation, I woke up, never to wear a "cape" again. Wherever the knowledge came from, it came nonetheless, and from that moment on I knew flying was nothing more than a childhood fantasy. I would never fly . . . and there is no Superman.

In retrospect, my day of "enlightenment" was a very sad day. I know now that something inside of me died that day. Whatever the "something" was, it was the stuff of dreams and imagination—the place where dancing, singing, laughter, and playing lived. Even at six, I understood that the possibility of flying wasn't the point: it was the aliveness I felt when I *thought* I could fly; it was the voice I heard deep inside—a warm and loving voice, a living, believing voice, a wild and dangerous voice. Every time I heard that voice, I recognized who it was: God. But that day, when I was just six years young, my God-hearing went bad.

There is, deep within *all* of us, a *voice*. It speaks to us continuously, knocking on the door of our consciousness. When we are children, the voice is very loud (as it was with me), shattering our awareness with overwhelming clarity. Its loudness is not like a train or jet engine. It shouts to us with a whisper. It is like the wind breezing through a field of daisies, scattering their petals across the sky into a flower snowstorm. It is like a thousand flutes echoing in the middle of the forest. This voice of our childhood is the voice of wonder and amazement, the voice of God, which has always been speaking to us, even before we were born.

One sad day, we are aware of an absence. We can no longer hear the God-voice, and we are left with only silence—not a quiet silence but a roaring silence.

We did not want to stop hearing God's voice. Indeed, God kept on speaking. But our lives became louder. The increasing crescendo of our possessions, the ear-piercing noise of busyness, and the soul-smothering volume of our endless activity drowned out the still, small voice of God.

Most of us cannot say *when* it happened, we only know *that* it happened. When we became aware of the absence of God's voice, there were a thousand deaths within us. Idealism and innocence died first. And across the scarred terrain of our souls, one could see the withered remains of dreams, spontaneity, poetry, passion, and ourselves—our *real* selves, the persons we were made to be.

What happened? What happened to our aliveness? How could we grow up, accumulate twelve to fifteen years of education (or more), get married, have children, work for decades, and never really *live*? How could we begin our lives with clarity and passion, wonder and spontaneity, yet so quickly find ourselves at the middle or end of our lives, dull and bleary-eyed, listless and passionless?

The death of the soul is never quick. It is a slow dying, a succession of little deaths that continues until we wake up one day on the edge of God's voice, on the fringe of God's belovedness, beyond the adventure of God's claim on our lives.

The place where I live, located under the shadow of Mount Shasta, is a valley spotted with leftover lava from long-ago volcanic eruptions. As a result, ranches (rather than farms) checker the terrain of Siskiyou County in northern California. Cattle ranches predominate, and cows are everywhere. Local range laws specify that if a cow wanders into the road and your car hits it, you are legally responsible for the animal's death. Many ranches have extensive fencing, but too many cows still manage to end up on the road. One morning I came across an old story told by a farmer which explains how cows end up on the road lost:

> A cow is nibbling on a tuft of grass in the middle of a field, moving from one tuft to the next, and before you know it he ends up at some grass next to the fence. Noticing a nice clump of green on the other side of the fence, the cow stumbles through an old tear in the fence and finds himself outside on the road. "Cows don't intend to get lost," the farmer explained, "they *just nibble their way to lostness!*"[1]

The farmer didn't know it, but he was talking about more than cows. None of us intends to wander from the green pasture of God's voice! None of us intends to have our souls wander onto the dull and listless highway of the American Way. First comes the tuft of education, then the tuft of marriage, then children, a new home, and one day we wake up to discover that we have nibbled our way to lostness.

It took me fifty years to realize I was lost. No one knew I was lost—my life had all the *trappings* of found-ness. I was a pastor, for heaven's sake. I had spent twenty-five years in church-related ministry, and most of my days were consumed with writing or talking about Jesus. And yet I was lost, confused, soul weary, thirsty, and bone tired. I had succeeded at mimicking aliveness, but I was nearly dead.

In desperation, I picked up a book by Henri Nouwen titled *In the Name of Jesus*. It is a small book. I read it in a couple of hours, but the reading of it was irrelevant. It was the ringing in my ears when I finished the book that commanded my attention. I had heard a familiar voice. Oh, it wasn't audible, *but I heard it nonetheless*. The voice was the voice of my childhood. It was the unmistakable voice of *Jesus*. He had found *me!* He had been hiding in the pages of Henri's book, and my heart began to tingle with anticipation. The numbness of my soul began to dissipate, and I could sense the beginning of a wild and new way of living. I was full of joy and fear at the same time because I knew that if I listened to this Jesus and followed Him—if I, like the disciples, left my fishing or my tax collecting—He would lead me into treacherous territory, where every day would be an experience of danger and wonder at the same time: an adventure of *dangerous wonder!*

I was correct. Five years ago I decided to start listening again to the voice of Jesus, and my life hasn't been the same since. He has not been telling me what to *do*, He has been telling me *how much He loves me*. He has not corrected my behavior, He has been leading me into His arms. And He has not protected me from the dangers of living, He has led me into the dangerous place of wild and terrifyingly wonder-*full* faith.

This book is called *Dangerous Wonder*. It is a book about the attributes of children that make childhood an adventure. When adults rediscover those attributes, when we re*claim* our childlikeness, we stumble upon the presence of God—and we are amazed to find the place all children know about: the place where we once again can hear the whisper of Jesus. Jesus always recognized children because they always recognized Him. When we find the place of dangerous wonder, our souls come to life and we sense that we are on the brink of a great and mysterious way of life.

I must warn you, this is not a book of principles or rules about how to live a happy Christian life. It is the almost illegible handwriting of a wide-eyed observer who can barely keep up with what he is seeing. The words in this book are not grand and magnificent. They are stuttering, irregular, broken, and tiny attempts to describe the adventure of a childlike faith. They're messy and lopsided—far from neat and orderly. Some of them may be irritating and annoying at times, like little children who interrupt our comfortable moments. May those words be a good annoyance, a welcome irritation, because I have discovered there is always the possibility of discovery just beyond irritation and annoyance.

This is an adventure book, written by a man who came precariously close to losing his childlike faith, and who is still in the midst of discovering how to be a child again. It is not a book of answers from someone who has arrived; it is merely glimpses from someone who is still stumbling around yet hot on God's trail.

Dangerous Wonder is meant to be a playful book. The chapter titles, the words, and the stories are all meant to play with your expectations. A counselor friend of mine is fond of saying, "When you do what you always do, you get what you always get." I have *purposely* tried to write an unpredictable book about God, using strange and unexpected words with the hope that you'll get what you didn't expect.

I hope you'll find Jesus unexpectedly hiding in the reading of this book, just as I found Him hiding in the writing of it. I hope, as you read, that you'll never be quite sure if you are chasing Jesus or if He is chasing you. In my experience, the good news is that when Jesus is near, who is chasing whom never seems to matter much.

My prayer is *not* that you will finish reading this book with great new intellectual understanding of the Christian faith; but rather, that somewhere in your reading you will hear the whisper of Jesus. And that somewhere in the pages of this book, you will feel stirring within you those childlike attributes of passion, curiosity, abandon, and wonder that are the source of Life itself. May the fire of Jesus' presence once again fill your every waking moment with passion and adventure!

Mike Yaconelli

CHAPTER ONE

Dangerous Wonder

We cover our deep ignorance with words,
but we are ashamed to wonder, we are afraid
to whisper "mystery."[1]

Sometimes I think the people to feel saddest for
are people who once knew what profoundness was, but who
lost or became numb to the sensation
of wonder.[2]

We live in a time when faith is thin,
because our aching for what is above and
beyond us has been anaesthetized and our capacity for
wonder reduced to clever tricks.[3]

I T WAS ONE OF THOSE SNOWFALLS YOU NEVER FORGET. MILLIONS of white flakes filled the air, quieting the earth and swallowing the sounds. The resulting silence was thick with a texture you could feel.

My nephew stood in the living room at the opening to our deck, a stranger to snow, his two years of life about to be altered irrevocably. His eyes were blank, unaware; his body clueless; his mind about to be overloaded with the electricity of discovery.

In the dark, Mother had maneuvered herself onto the deck's two feet of snow to capture the event on video. Dad manned the sliding door, which had been unlatched for quick opening into the darkness. Uncle's hands were poised on the switch to light the deck. And Aunt was ready to lift her nephew into the mysterious new world of twinkling ice and frozen softness.

The moment arrived.

In a perfectly timed instant the deck lights went on, the camera started recording, the sliding door swept open, and a two-year-old was transported from the world he knew to a world he had never seen.

Wonder filled the air.

His eyes stretched wide with astonishment, as though the only way to apprehend what he was seeing was for his eyes to become big enough to *contain it all*. He stood motionless, paralyzed. It was too much for a two-year-old, too much for an any-year-old (too often, when a person gets older, the person's "too-much detector" malfunctions, corroded by busyness and technology). He twitched and jerked each time a snowflake landed on his face, feeling it tingle as it was transformed from hostile cold to friendly warmth, caressing his face with tiny droplets of water. Just behind his large eyes you could see sparks flying from the crosscurrents of millions of electric stimuli overwhelming the circuit breakers of his previously small world. His mind was a confusion of strange, conflicting realities: *white, cold, floating, flying, tingling, electric, landing, touching, sparkling, melting*—causing an overload so great, so overwhelming, he fell backward—a slow-motion landing in the billowy whiteness, the snow tenderly embracing him. He had given up trying to understand snow and had given in to *experiencing* snow.

It was a moment of *wonder*.

The more I think about it, it was a moment of *dangerous* wonder. My nephew's awe and wonder caused him to surrender to the snow by falling into it. For a few magical seconds, the *danger* of snow had given way to the *wonder* of snow. For a brief moment my nephew came face-to-face with life at its fullest. He didn't know whether to cry or laugh, to be afraid or happy. My nephew experienced what it must have been like that first moment in Eden when Adam and Eve's eyes could not comprehend the staggering beauty of God's new creation. He experienced what it must have been like when the scales fell from the blind man's eyes and the explosion of color and shapes bombarded his mind for the first time; when the leper felt a surge of electricity through his body, his dead and rotting skin suddenly transformed into the fresh skin of a baby; when the bitter, hopeless prostitute looked up fully expecting judgment and death and instead heard the words of forgiveness and life.

What moments! What holy moments! To be in the presence of God, frightened and amazed at the same time! To feel as if you are in the presence of Life itself, yet with your soul shaking in both terror and gratitude.

I want a lifetime of holy moments. Every day I want to be in dangerous proximity to Jesus. I long for a life that explodes with meaning and is filled with adventure, wonder, risk, and *danger*. I long for a faith that is gloriously treacherous. I want to be with Jesus, not knowing whether to cry or laugh.

If I'm honest, most of my longings have been unfulfilled, and my living, very *un*treacherous . . . until a few years ago.

In 1991, my wife and I spent a week in a L'Arche community called Daybreak, where the majority of the members of the community are mentally and physically challenged. Many times during our stay, people in the community reminded me of little children. They were childlike. And what surprised me was how much the L'Arche community taught me about Jesus. I shouldn't have been surprised. Matthew 18:3 describes an incident in Jesus' life when He called a little child to come close to Him and then said to the adults in the audience, "I tell you the truth, unless you change and become like little children, you will never enter the kingdom of heaven." *It was true*. This wonderful community of people—who had *not* had their childlike attributes taken from them—gently guided me back to the place of danger and wonder.

What would happen if we all took Jesus' advice and "became like little children"—like my nephew? Is dangerous wonder a possibility for you and me? I believe it is. Why, then, don't more of us experience life in this way? Because we allow obstacles to squelch our wonder and steal our souls.

THE OBSTACLE OF DULLNESS

Episcopal priest Robert Capon named the first obstacle: "We are in a war between dullness and astonishment."[4] The most critical issue facing Christians is not abortion, pornography, the disintegration of the family, moral absolutes, MTV, drugs, racism, sexuality, or school prayer. *The critical issue today is dullness*. We have lost our astonishment. The Good News is no longer good news, it is okay news. Christianity is no longer life *changing*, it is life *enhancing*. Jesus doesn't change people into wild-eyed radicals anymore, He changes them into "nice people."

If Christianity is simply about being nice, I'm not interested.

What happened to radical Christianity, the un-nice brand of Christianity that turned the world upside-down? What happened to the category-smashing, life-threatening, anti-institutional gospel that spread through the first century like wildfire and was considered (by those in power) *dangerous?* What happened to the kind of Christians whose hearts were on fire, who had no fear, who spoke the truth no matter what the consequence, who made the world uncomfortable, who were willing to follow Jesus wherever He went? What happened to the kind of Christians who were filled with passion and gratitude, and who every day were unable to get over the grace of God?

I'm ready for a Christianity that "ruins"[5] my life, that captures my heart and makes me uncomfortable. I want to be filled with an astonishment which is so captivating that I am considered wild and unpredictable and . . . well . . . *dangerous.* Yes, I want to be "dangerous" to a dull and boring religion. I want a faith that is considered "dangerous" by our predictable and monotonous culture.

A. W. Tozer said a long time ago, "Culture is putting out the light in men and women's souls."[6] He was right. Dullness is more than a religious issue, it is a cultural issue. Our entire culture has become dull. Dullness is the absence of the light of our souls. Look around. We have lost the sparkle in our eyes, the passion in our marriages, the meaning in our work, the joy of our faith.

The Bible names our problem: *sin.* Don't let the word fool you. Sin is more than turning our backs on God, it is turning our backs on *life!* Immorality is much more than adultery and dishonesty it is living *drab, colorless, dreary, stale, unimaginative lives.* The greatest enemy of Christianity may be people who say they believe in Jesus but *who are no longer astonished and amazed.* Jesus Christ came to rescue us from listlessness as well as lostness; He came to save us from flat souls as well as corrupted souls. He came to save us from dullness. Our culture is awash in immorality and drowning in dullness. We have forgotten how to dance, how to sing, and how to laugh. We have allowed technology to beat our imaginations into submission and have become tourists rather than travelers. Television dominates our time, alters our values, numbs us to life in all of its wildness. We have been stunted by mediocrity.

THE OBSTACLE OF THE DREAM STEALERS

Somewhere along the way we had the child chased out of us. Our childlikeness is usually snuffed out by people who tell us what we *can't* do. They are dream stealers.

My first year of Bible college was a nightmare. Naive, immature, and wildly enthusiastic about my faith, I quickly became active in all the college events. My friends and I signed up for the campus talent show and worked for two months on a very difficult jazz arrangement of "Moonglow." Everyone who heard us practice was impressed. The applause in the rehearsal hall was deafening when we finished tryouts, and we were sure we'd made the performance. Abruptly, we were called outside by a lanky, harsh-looking man. "I'm sorry," he said, "but you will not be able to perform tomorrow night. Your song is too worldly. It sounds too much like a song that would be sung in a nightclub."

"What?!" I responded. *"But we're not in a nightclub, we're at a Christian school!"*

"The decision is final," he said and walked away.

Our group was crushed. I never recovered. My enthusiasm was gone, and I withdrew from all activities. For reasons I still do not understand, the teachers at this college proudly lived out their roles as dream stealers.

Jack Canfield tells about a young high school student whose father was a horse trainer. Because the family had to follow the horse-racing season, the young boy had to change schools throughout the year. During his senior year he was asked to write a paper about what his dreams for the future were. His paper described his dream of owning a 200-acre horse ranch with stables and tracks, and a 4,000-square-foot home. He even drew a diagram of the property and the design of his house. He turned the paper in . . . and two days later it came back with an "F" on the front and a note to see the teacher. After class, the teacher explained to the boy that his dream was "unrealistic." The teacher said that if the boy rewrote the paper with a much more realistic dream, he would reconsider the grade. The boy went home and asked his father what to do. "It's your decision," said the father. Dad knew this was a very important decision. The boy kept the paper for a week and then returned it to his teacher after class. "Here," the boy said, "you can keep the 'F' and I'll keep my dream."[7]

That teacher was another dream stealer.

During his first year of college, a young man I know became clinically depressed and decided to take a break from school. The boy's father, who was quite wealthy, tried to convince him to stay in school, but to no avail. Instead the young man went to the mission field, and his life turned around. He went off his anti-depressant medication and soon decided to follow Christ to a dangerous and politically unstable country. His mother was thrilled, but the father went ballistic. Threatening to sue the mission organization, the father harassed and verbally abused his son to the point of broken-ness. The depression returned.

This father was a dream stealer.

Interestingly, the Bible has a name for religious dream stealers—Pharisees.

A man was blind from birth and Jesus gave him his dream of sight. The dream-stealing Pharisees did everything to rob that man of his dream (John 9).

A woman with a questionable reputation poured expensive perfume on Jesus, and the dream stealers in the room tried to steal from her the joy of gratitude (Mark 14).

Matthew's gospel (see 12:1-8) also gives us an example. Christ's disciples, new to the faith, were giddy with the exhilaration of following Jesus. They were clueless and naive, filled with awe and wonder. Hungry, they begin to tromp through a field picking food to eat. Suddenly their reverie is broken by Pharisees yelling, "WHAT ARE YOU DOING? You are not to work on the Sabbath! Religion is about rules and regulations and you are acting irresponsibly."

Dream stealers.

They might as well have said, "Look, religion should not make you full of life, it should be serious business. Religion is all about rules and regulations. Learn where the lines are. Now, obey the Sabbath and behave like the rest of us and we'll give you another chance." In effect Jesus said to them, "You can have your rules. I'll keep giving people their dream of an adventurous faith!" Christ is the Dream Giver who wants us to listen to His dream for us so we can run like children in the fields of His grace. Trouble is, the fields are full of obstacles—obstacles that deafen us to God's dreams for us and keep us from an adventurous faith.

THE OBSTACLE OF PREDICTABILITY

Something happens in a technological society—first identified, by the way, in 1964 by a French Christian, Jacques Ellul (*The Technological Society*, Vintage Press). Ellul predicted that the emergence of technology would alter the nature of life as we know it, just as the Industrial Revolution did. First man and nature, then man and machine, and now, just machine. Technology would become autonomous, and soon, rather than man controlling machine, machine would control and *define* man. Not only would hamburgers and health care be franchised, but human beings would be franchised, first by an *exterior* cloning and then by genetic cloning.

He was right. Even genetic cloning is upon us. But *cultural* cloning is even more harmful to our souls. It levels human personality and deifies predictability. When this is the goal, diversity is no longer recognized as a strength in this culture. Sameness becomes the bottom line.

Predictability and faith cannot coexist. What characterized Jesus and His disciples was *unpredictability*. Jesus was
always surprising the disciples by eating at the wrong houses
(those of sinners), hanging around the wrong people (tax collectors, adulterers, prostitutes, lepers), and healing people on
the wrong day (the Sabbath). There was no Day Timer ™, no
strategic plan, no mission statement; there was only the eager
anticipation of the present moment. The Pharisees wanted
Jesus to be the *same* as they were. His truth should be the same
truth that they had spent centuries taming. But truth is *un*predictable. When Jesus is present, everyone is uncomfortable
yet mysteriously glad at the same time. People do not like
surprises—even church people—and they don't want to be
uncomfortable. They want a nice, tame Jesus.

You know what? Tameness is not an option.

Take surprise out of faith and all that is left is dry and
dead religion. Take away mystery from the gospel and all that
is left is a frozen and petrified dogma. Lose your awe of God
and you are left with an impotent deity. Abandon astonishment
and you are left with meaningless piety. When religion is characterized by sameness, when faith is franchised, when the
genuineness of our experience with God is evaluated by its
similarities to others' faith, then the uniqueness of God's people
is dead and the church is lost.

THE OBSTACLE OF THE BANAL

Most of us act as if it is more important to make a living than
to live. Financial security is much more valued than the insecurity of following Christ. Most people would tell us that
money, not poverty, matters. Even in the church, well-meaning
Christians would advise fellow Christians to seek financial
security. Seek Christ, yes, but don't be foolhardy, don't be silly,
don't be childish. Find a good job. You can serve God and still
work for a standard of living that reflects the economic realities
of today. Frederick Buechner warns us about such thinking:

The danger is that you will not listen to the voice that speaks to you through the seagull mounting the gray wind, say, or the vision in the temple, that you do not listen to the voice inside you or to the voice that speaks from outside but specifically to you out of the specific events of your life, but that instead you listen to the great blaring, boring, banal voice of our mass culture, which threatens to deafen us all by blasting forth that the only thing that really matters about your work is how much it will get you in the way of salary and status, and that if it is gladness you are after, you can save that for weekends.[8]

Jesus called His disciples to a very odd standard of living — nothing. Obviously, childlike faith is faith that trusts Jesus' standard of living (seek ye first the kingdom of God) instead of the modern society's standard of living (seek ye first the kingdom of things).[9] When our possessions possess us — imprison us — risk and adventure become impossible.

RECAPTURING DANGEROUS WONDER

The result? We have lost the gleam in our eye. Jesus no longer chases us in the ragged terrain of our souls. We have forgotten what it is like to stand speechless in the presence of Jesus, hearts beating wildly, staggered and stunned by what God is doing in our world. The obstacles are intimidating, but they need not dictate our lives. We can rediscover the childlike attribute of our faith called dangerous wonder.

Do not give up. Dangerous wonder is still possible for us all. You can still experience a volatile mix of astonishment and terror, awe and risk, amazement and fear, adventure and exhilaration, tears and laughter, passion and anticipation, daring and enchantment.

Let me remind you of two instances of dangerous wonder. Mary was a young woman, a teenager, a virgin betrothed to be married to a young kid in town, Joseph, a virgin as well. Nazareth was a small town, Joseph's dad was a carpenter, and the young Mary and Joseph were cute and respected by all who knew them. Life was looking good for this youthful couple.

Everyone was looking forward to the wedding. And then an angel showed up. Have you ever wondered why every time an angel shows up in the Bible, the first words out of its mouth are "Fear not!"? The angel announced to Mary that she had found "favor with God" because she was pregnant (some *favor*). Great news, all right. How do you explain this one to your fiancé? Instead of a wonderful wedding, the blessing of the community, and a nice predictable life, Joseph and Mary began a nightmarish adventure.

Joseph had to embrace a pregnancy that wasn't his; both of them had to flee the country and live in exile; and they had to deal emotionally with the reality that, because of their baby, many innocent babies were slaughtered. Joseph and Mary experienced the dangerous wonder of following an unpredictable God. My hunch is that they never regretted their lives.

Another instance occurs one night when the disciples were rowing across a lake while Jesus slept in the stern of the boat. A frightening storm surprised them, and before they could prepare, their old and questionable boat was being slammed by ten-foot swells, they were taking in water, and they were in danger of sinking. The disciples were terrified and finally woke Jesus up, screaming in desperation, "We're going to drown!" They must have been thinking, *Hey, You are the Son of God. You made storms! Do something!*

Jesus did do something. He said, "Be still!" And the storm stopped. The water was immediately as calm as glass. It was eerily still. I have to believe the disciples were petrified. I'll bet they didn't move for thirty minutes until, finally, one of them leaned over to the others and said, "Don't make Him mad." I believe the disciples were more afraid *after* the storm was calmed than during it. The disciples experienced firsthand the dangerous wonder of being with Jesus.

Do you want to be just like Jesus? The Jesus of the New Testament was a long way from dull—crying one minute and knocking over tables the next; showing courageous compassion to a fallen victim one day and cursing hypocrites the next; blasting the Pharisees one day for having such a narrow view of adultery, then on the next day forgiving a woman caught in adultery. The New Testament writers continually describe the crowds as responding to Jesus with amazement.

Jesus was a dangerous man—dangerous to the power structure, dangerous to the church, dangerous to the crowds of people who followed Him.

Shouldn't the *followers* of Christ also be dangerous? Shouldn't everyone be awed and dazzled by Christians? Shouldn't Christians be known by the fire in their souls, the wild-eyed gratitude in their faces, the twinkle in their eyes, and a holy mischief in their demeanors? Shouldn't Christianity be considered dangerous—unpredictable, threatening to the status quo, living outside the lines, uncontrollable, fearless, wild, beyond categorization or definition? Shouldn't those who call themselves Christians be filled with awe, astonishment, and amazement?

Let's find the world of dangerous wonder. It's a real place, you know. It is the place where both children and grownups can find God, located just beyond where the sidewalk ends. The directions just might be found in the pages of this book. Dull people and dream stealers are not welcome. It is a place like Narnia in *The Lion, the Witch, and the Wardrobe*, when Aslan has come back from death. Lucy and the children, eyes wide open with astonishment, recognize him, and then Aslan says,

"And now—"

"Oh yes. Now?" said Lucy jumping up and clapping her hands.

"Oh, children," said the Lion, "I feel my strength coming back to me. Oh, children, catch me if you can!"

He stood for a second, his eyes very bright, his limbs

quivering, lashing himself with his tail. Then he made
a leap high over their heads and landed on the other
side of the table. Laughing, though she didn't know
why, Lucy scrambled over it to reach him. Aslan leaped
again. A mad chase began. Round and round the hill-
top he led them, now hopelessly out of their reach,
now letting them almost catch his tail, now diving
between them, now tossing them in the air with his
huge and beautifully velveted paws and catching them
again, and now stopping unexpectedly so that all three
of them rolled over together in a happy laughing heap
of fur and arms and legs. It was such a romp as no one
has ever had except in Narnia, and whether it was
more like playing with a thunderstorm or playing with
a kitten Lucy could never make up her mind. And the
funny thing was that when all three finally lay together
panting in the sun the girls no longer felt in the least
tired or hungry or thirsty.[10]

It is time to find the place where the dangerous wonder of
faith can be discovered—a place landscaped by risky curiosity, wild abandon, daring playfulness, quiet listening, irresponsible passion, happy terror, and naive grace.

In a day when most of us are tired, worn-out, thirsty, and
starving for life and joy and peace, maybe it is time to become
a child again. Maybe it is time to quit college and take a year
off to go to the mission field, or give up a secure job and go back
to school, or leave the corporation because the work is killing
our souls, or give up the possessions that are possessing us.

Maybe it *is* time to live this dangerous wonder of faith, take
our shoes off, roll up our sleeves, and have "such a romp as no
one has ever seen." Maybe it's time to play in the snow once
again.

CHAPTER TWO

Risky Curiosity

*In every mind there is an enormous store
of not-knowing, of being puzzled, of wonder,
of radical amazement.*[1]

Doubt is the shadow cast by faith.[2]

*Risk, as we have seen, is indispensable to any significant
life, nowhere more clearly than in the life of the spirit. The
goal of faith is not to create a set of immutable,
rationalized, precisely defined and defendable beliefs to
preserve forever.
It is to recover a relationship with God.*[3]

THERE IS A POINT IN A CHILD'S DEVELOPMENT WHEN THE CHILD'S mind seems shaped like a question mark—every sentence begins with "why." The answers seem only to raise more questions. Most parents understand that although it is important to attempt an answer, often the answer is irrelevant. For little children, *what is most important is the act of questioning itself* because children's questions are more than a request for information. Their questions are an act of affection, of communion, and of trusting.

In a healthy family, children's questions are not about answers—their questions are about relationship. Children intuitively know their questions are welcome, appreciated. Safe. And not only are children's *questions* welcome, but *they* are welcome. In a welcoming environment where questions are safe, children are infected with *curiosity*—a fascination with truth, an unrelenting hunger to know and *be known*, to capture and be captured, to touch and be touched. When these children finally fall asleep at night, they are secure in the knowledge that the one who loves them is bigger than all their questions. They can sleep deeply, knowing they are safe in the arms of the Keeper of their questions.

C. S. Lewis described Aslan, the Christ figure in the *Chronicles of Narnia*, as a "not so tame lion." The reason so many of us have lost our childhood curiosity is that we've been *tamed*. Our world is populated with domesticated grownups who would rather settle for safe, predictable answers instead of wild, unpredictable mystery. Faith has been reduced to a comfortable system of *beliefs* about God instead of an *un*comfortable encounter *with* God. Childlike faith understands that God is as capable of destroying us as He is of saving us. Risky curiosity breaks from the safety and

35

comfort of a tame faith and ventures into the terrifying presence of a "not so tame" God.

Thomas, one of Jesus' disciples, is best known for his childlike curiosity. Thomas believed in Jesus, trusted Him, followed Him, was willing to die for Him, but he was infected with a risky curiosity. When everyone else said they had seen Jesus after the Crucifixion, Thomas wasn't satisfied. He wanted more. He wanted to touch Jesus, hear Jesus, see Jesus, embrace Him. Most theologians have labeled Thomas a doubter. "Doubting Thomas" is the negative spin they have applied to Thomas's questioning. I disagree. Thomas wasn't doubting Jesus, he was longing for Jesus. Curiosity is a hunger of the soul, and because Thomas was strong and courageous and spoke bluntly, he was daring enough to ask tough questions. He was not refusing to believe, he was refusing to settle for secondhand faith. Thomas was driven to *know* truth—to mingle with it, wrestle with it, become intimate with it. Jesus didn't criticize Thomas. He honored his curiosity. Jesus legitimized Thomas's holy curiosity.

Childlike faith looks a lot like the faith of Thomas—daring, reckless, bold, and aggressive.

A friend of mine spent the last year in and out of the hospital; the combination of a failing heart and cancer was almost too much to bear. His courage and determination caused him to bounce back from the edge of death, and he and his wife were able to celebrate Christmas together at home. I suggested we celebrate Communion in their home on Christmas Day. Just before the appointed time, they called and asked if we could wait another hour because their grandson, his girlfriend, and her two boys from a previous marriage would like to take Communion as well. I walked into their small home to find everyone seated at the dining room table—Grandma and Grandpa filled with anticipation; Grandson, girlfriend, and two boys noticeably nervous.

After placing the bread and wine on the table, I asked if there were any questions before we started. The eleven-year-old boy,

Joshua, asked if he could sit in on the Communion. "Of course," I said and checked to see if his mother agreed. She did. After the words of institution, I began to pass the bread and wine around the group.

"May I take Communion?" Joshua asked.

"Sure," I said. "Do you understand what all of this means?"

The grandson interrupted, "Yes, he does. I explained it to him."

Joshua took the body and blood of Christ, and as I was preparing to say the final prayer, he blurted out, "Sir, how can you hear God speak to you?"

Where this question came from I have no idea. I paused for a minute and said, "Well, Joshua, if you listen very carefully, you will know when God speaks to you. It may not be an audible voice, or it might not happen right away. But if you really listen, you will hear God speak." The trouble with children is they believe you. Immediately Joshua squeezed his eyes, scrunched his body into listening mode, and started listening. I had given Joshua the adult answer to his question, never expecting him to put the answer to the test so soon.

"I heard Him!" Joshua yelled. "I heard God speak!"

I honestly don't think any of us in the room really believed Joshua heard God speak. We were trying to be nice, but we weren't expecting God to actually show up. "What did He say?" I asked. I was patronizing him, fully expecting some childish response.

Joshua looked straight into my eyes, his own eyes wide with wonder. "He said, *'Don't forget Me!'*" A boy's risky curiosity had brought him into the presence of God.

DARING FAITH

When children ask questions, they are not afraid to interrupt, irritate, or interrogate until someone responds. Children are born with a natural curiosity and built-in daring. It doesn't take long before our culture explains to them the "inappropriateness" of curiosity in the "real" world, and their naive courage is intimidated out of them. By the time most of our children reach junior high school, their natural curiosity has been neutralized by an insidious set of unwritten assumptions:

Assumption 1: *Questions can be embarrassing.* According to this assumption, it's embarrassing to admit you don't know something. What is important is never to *reveal* your ignorance. Don't *admit* you don't know something because others may think less of you. In today's world, truth doesn't matter. Image does. Silence your doubts, ignore your questions, don't do anything that might cause someone to think ill of you. As Flannery O'Connor reminded us, "mystery is the great embarrassment to the modern mind."[4]

Assumption 2: *Questions can make people uncomfortable.* Questions can cause others to question. Our doubts might resonate with others' doubts. Because of our questions, others might have to face questions they have learned to ignore. Questions force us to think, to struggle, to interact with truth. In other words, the act of questioning is discomforting. Many Christians have silenced their questions; they've ignored the gaps in their thinking and don't want those questions reawakened.

Assumption 3: *Questions can be dangerous.* Many in our culture have opted to stay safe by limiting our knowledge to what we already know—a self-induced retirement of the mind. If we ask too many questions, the resulting answers might cause us to change. We might become accountable for truth and have to act on it. The Pharisees wanted to shut up Jesus for good. His constant questions were threatening to the status quo. Jesus' questions were dangerous because the very asking of them was eroding the power structure. Jesus had to be killed because He had to be *silenced*. Asking "who is my neighbor?" (Luke 10:29) and "whose image is on this coin?" (see Mark 12:16) can cause a riot. It's better not to ask, according to this rule.

Assumption 4: *Questions can be "right" or "wrong."* All of us have had the experience of asking a question, only to be told the question was inappropriate, irrelevant, or "wrong." According to this rule, "wrong" questions reveal a lack of faith, a refusal to believe, a rebellion, a carnal heart. "Wrong" questions are unanswerable questions. "Wrong" questions threaten the majority viewpoint.

These unwritten rules have saturated the church and have resulted in pews full of weak, anemic Christians who have stifled their curiosity and who suffer from a withering faith.

RISKY CURIOSITY

There are no "wrong" questions. When people are hungry for God, every question is "right." Curiosity is the unknown fruit of the Spirit, the stealthy expression of God's presence. Faith opens our eyes and brings us face-to-face with a new reality—a reality rich with new vistas of knowing. Thomas was willing to defy a roomful of disciples with his bold curiosity. Daring and unafraid, he stood up to his peers and refused to base his relationship with Jesus on the displeasure of others. What stopped Thomas in his tracks was the willingness of Jesus to honor his risky curiosity. Jesus had already appeared to the disciples once, but He came back a week later and spoke directly to Thomas and told Thomas to touch Him so Thomas's questioning could stop and his believing could begin. Curiosity is welcome in the presence of Jesus even when it is not welcome anywhere else.

I pastor a small church in a rural community in northern California's Siskiyou Mountains. With only thirty or so in attendance each Sunday, it is difficult for a person to hide or go unnoticed. Maria, one of the small group of teenagers who attend, makes herself known every Sunday. Sometime during the sermon, I can expect to look out at the congregation and see Maria with her hand raised. I stop my sermon and recognize Maria. Her comment is always a form of this question: "Mike, what the heck are you talking about?"

Maria is naive enough to believe she should understand the sermon *before* she leaves church. I can see the look of relief on the faces of all the adults who are thinking the same question *but are afraid to interrupt*. Maria's curiosity is still alive and well when everyone else's has been silenced. Maria is willing to dare and willing to suffer the irritation of others who would prefer that the sermon be over on time. Maria is strangely and wonderfully unaffected by the dismay of others, including this minister, who must then explain what I mean instead of assuming I am understood. Maria's childlike, risky curiosity has resulted in sermons which are interactive instead of entertaining. Truth is being worked out, not just listened to.

COURAGEOUS FAITH

Curiosity requires courage. You must be willing to ask questions even when they threaten everyone around you. Faith is more than believing; it is an act of courage, a bold grasping of God's truth. Faith is a wrestling match with God, an intense struggle with truth in an attempt to squeeze every bit of knowledge out of it. Curiosity is the shape of our hunger for God. We question God without apology, we march into the presence of God bringing our armfuls of questions — without fear — because God is not afraid of them. People are afraid. Institutions are afraid. But God is not.

Children are possessed with certain inalienable rights, and one of them is the right to ask questions anytime and anywhere. We have these same rights because we are the children of God. Let us ask our questions boldly, courageously, like a little child.

LONELY FAITH

People who ask questions isolate themselves. Just look at Thomas. I can understand the disciples' frustration with Thomas's questions. They had seen Jesus and experienced His presence, so why couldn't Thomas take their word for it? Didn't he trust his friends? Was he jealous? Was he envious of their firsthand experience? Thomas's questions isolated him from the rest of the disciples and probably would have had a long-term effect on their relationship if it hadn't been for Jesus. Jesus wasn't offended by Thomas's curiosity. The disciples may have isolated him, but Jesus *included* him. Jesus "showed up" at the point of Thomas's curiosity. Our questions may chase everyone else away, but they attract Jesus. We may be stuck with our questions, but we are also stuck with Jesus. If our questions leave us alone with Jesus, then lonely isn't a bad place to be.

UNKNOWING FAITH

Think back to those times when a child you knew was curious about the moon, a snake, Grandma's wrinkles, or your bald head. Remember how you tried to answer the questions, knowing the little girl standing next to you could not grasp your answer? Yet patiently (or impatiently) you attempted an answer. To your amazement the child looked at you and said, "Oh. Thanks." Off she went, anxious to run outside, no more enlightened than when the question was asked, but *it didn't seem to matter.*

A child's question is never exclusively about the moon or wrinkles. The question of a child is a million questions: Do you love me? Do I matter? Do you care about me? Do you want me to grow? Is what I notice worth noticing? Is Grandmother okay? Do you have a disease? Am I going to look like you? Is my hair going to fall out like yours?[5] Parents have two primary responsibilities when it comes to children's questions—the very same responsibilities the church has for the people of faith:

Treasuring the Questions

When parents understand their role, they understand that they do not exist to answer every question their children have. Parents must help children discern the *important* questions, the life-giving questions.[6] Christianity must do the same. Alan Jones says that priests "are not so much people with answers as ones who guard the important questions and keep them alive."[7] The church exists to guard the important questions![8] Keep them alive! When the questions are kept alive, our souls have a chance of staying alive. The church should be full of Christians who seek questions rather than answers, mystery instead of solutions, wonder instead of explanations.

The Power of Unknowing

The ancient church fathers used to talk freely of "unknowing." It was their contention that the end of knowledge had much to teach us. They believed we could learn as much about God in what we *didn't* know as in what we did know. Our inability to answer all the questions became an opportunity to learn more about God. When our intellect fell short, our souls connected with the reality of God. There, in our unknowing, God showed up unexpectedly.

When our daughter, Lisa, was diagnosed with cancer at eighteen months old, she made many friends at Children's Hospital in San Diego. All of her friends at Children's had some catastrophic disease or illness. Once a week Lisa, along with a number of her friends, would line up to receive their "meds," or chemotherapy shots. Up until this time I thought I knew all there was to know about prayer. Standing in line with eight other children who had cancer, I discovered I knew nothing about prayer. How could I pray for my daughter's healing when eight other children needed healing, too? What was I asking—that God heal my daughter and ignore the others? Because I was a Christian, was my daughter exempt from dying? From that moment on, I knew less about prayer . . . and in some mystical way, I knew *more* about prayer. Even though my daughter's healing was no longer central to prayer, I was brought closer to Jesus in a way I didn't understand; and because I no longer "understood" prayer, I was able to sense God's presence in a way that I had never experienced before. Childlike faith is a faith that longs for God and seeks Him wherever He may be—even in the place of no answers.

THE MAGIC OF "WHY?"

In the last chapter I mentioned that Karla and I spent a week at Daybreak Retreat Center. We were soul weary. We had come to the point where our busy lives were "putting our souls in danger."⁹ Desperate for our souls to be mended, we gathered in the bitter December cold for our first meeting. We had come with a group of our friends and were anxious to meet Henri Nouwen and Sue Mosteller, the leaders of our retreat.

The first meeting brought together our group of eight, three workers at L'Arche, and three mentally and/or physically challenged residents of the community. I had read many of Henri Nouwen's books and fully expected his remarks at our first meeting to be life changing. During the obligatory introductions, I had admitted to the group that my busyness was draining my soul of life—leaving it lifeless and weak. Although Henri's opening remarks were interesting, I was disappointed. I expected profound insights. What I received was the logistical instructions for the week.

After the meeting, somewhat dismayed, I was confronted by a handsome resident of L'Arche. I'll call him Robert. Robert was in his forties, and although his appearance was normal, his vocabulary wasn't—it was limited to maybe a few hundred words. He stood uncomfortably close, his face within inches of mine. With his eyes focused directly on mine he said, "Busy?"

Startled with his concise summary of what I had admitted earlier, I said patronizingly, "Yes, Robert, I'm very busy."

"Too busy?" he continued.

"Yes, Robert," I admitted rather sheepishly, "I am too busy."

I will never forget what happened next. He moved even closer (his eyes revealing his sadness for me) and asked with a sincerity I have seldom experienced, *"Why?"*

My eyes filled with tears. Robert, a man with a very limited vocabulary, had asked the one question I had been afraid to ask. Somehow he knew that the solution to my weariness was hidden somewhere in the answer to his question—a question I was afraid to ask and no one else had. Why was I so busy? Because I still was hanging on to the belief that God's affection for me was measured by my activity for Him. The more things I did for God, the more He would love me, or so my insecurities kept telling me. Robert, in his childlike way, could see my insecurity, could feel my need to prove to God I was worth loving. By asking me a simple question, Robert started me on a journey toward intimacy with my Father. Amazingly, Robert's risky curiosity peered deep into my soul, enabling me to begin hearing what God had been spending my lifetime trying to say to me: "I love you, Michael, questions and all, with an unconditional, no-strings-attached love."

THE GOD BEYOND OUR QUESTIONS

I had retreated to the Oregon coast to be alone. The questions of my faith were draining the life out of me and I desperately needed solitude. One afternoon I took a walk to the edge of the Oregon coast. The sky was dark and menacing, the wind strong and wild, the water crashing against the rocks, chaotic, and deafening. *Thunderous!*

There I stood, inches away from the life-threatening waters, and I was frightened.

And yet, I was covered with a gentle mist, soothing my soul, and silently awakening me to a presence. There He was, in the eye of the stormy waters, asking me to come to Him. His gentleness was only perceptible because of the roaring waters around me. Give me a Jesus who meets me in the rushing, crashing waters of my questions. Let me stand precariously close to the dark and menacing skies of doubt, so I can hear the fierce and gentle loving voice of my Jesus who drowns out my fears and stands just beyond my questions with open arms.

CHAPTER THREE

Wild Abandon

Mistaking this active life of faith for an institutionally backed and culturally bound belief system is similar to reducing the Mona Lisa to paint-by-numbers.[1]

The living Jesus is a problem in our religious institutions. Yes. Because if you are having a funeral, a nice funeral, and the dead person starts to move, there goes the funeral! And, dear brothers and sisters, Jesus is moving![2]

IT WAS THE '50s—1952 TO BE EXACT. AT TEN YEARS OLD, MY everyday agenda had one focus—playing. Each day would bring a new challenge as my friends and I determined what activity would capture our attention. We lived in a lower economic neighborhood populated with hundreds of children who never felt poor, never thought about what we didn't have, what we were "deprived" of. We only knew that the options for playing were endless—marbles, street stickball tournaments, Ping-Pong championships, hide-and-seek, squirt-gun fights, swimming at the city pool, riding our bikes to the sugar beet factory, exploring boxcars at isolated train tracks. There were no televisions to distract us (most of our families couldn't afford one), no video games to swallow up the time. All we had was our imaginations.

Looking back at those years, I realize our imaginations were more than enough to keep us busy and make us wish the days were longer. Oh, there were some hot July days in southern California when our energy was sapped and we would complain about "nothing to do." Our parents were not very sympathetic. "There is plenty to do!" they would point out. "And if you can't find anything to do, we have some chores you can do." It didn't take long for us to occupy ourselves.

One July morning as my friends and I were sitting around on our bikes, daydreaming about what might be that day's adventure, Jimmy blurted out, "Let's build a spaceship!" The moment the words left his mouth, we knew destiny had spoken. Three boys on Evergreen Street were to build a spaceship. No one said a word, yet it was clear what we were to do. Our assignments were obvious; we knew instinctively who would do what. Jimmy, the ham operator's son, would be the communications officer and in charge of the radio and engineering components. I was in charge of the spaceship structure—my dad worked at Sears, a great source of rocket shells, otherwise known as refrigerator boxes. I was also the captain. Alan was in charge of logistics—his dad was in construction and Alan was very strong. He was also the navigator.

The construction of the spaceship took three full days. My backyard was chosen as the launchpad and subsequent space location, much to my parents' chagrin. It took two days to haul the exterior of the spaceship into place, another day to construct its interior, and then one full day to familiarize ourselves with our new surroundings so that everyone knew his role and was comfortable with his section of the spaceship, and to ensure that all the commands and destinations were mapped out and understood.

We were the envy of the neighborhood, with space voyages occurring daily for weeks. I don't remember how many weeks because, while our spaceship was "operational," we were oblivious to time. Every morning we could hardly wait to get done with our chores and be back in the spaceship. The time went by quickly. For most of the summer our world was our spaceship, where we miraculously survived meteor attacks, intergalactic battles with alien enemies, internal explosions, attempted mutinies, and mysterious forces of evil. There were many other crises we managed to overcome—Jimmy was grounded for a week when it was discovered he had equipped his communications center with his dad's most expensive equipment (after he had spent a week searching his garage for it!). Then there was the rainstorm that weakened the boxes to the point of collapse, followed by the attack of the St. Bernard on the navigator's room. (The navigator was so angry he threatened to quit, so we had to take two days to find a new refrigerator box and help him rebuild his section of the spaceship.)

I'll never forget the day our magical space voyage ended. Apparently, all of our parents met secretly the night before and decided it was time for the spaceship to be dismantled. The lawn under the spaceship was dead, the boxes were caving in after too many dew-filled evenings, and school would be starting in two weeks. We couldn't believe how much debris our spaceship had accumulated over the summer. It took us five full days to rid ourselves of the junk we had collected and to clean up the mess.

What I remember most about my days as captain of our neighborhood spaceship is the wild abandon I experienced. While the spaceship was active, our schedules, our relationships, all of our personal responsibilities fell under the shadow of our imaginary space voyage. Our every waking moment was consumed with the spaceship. By the end of the summer, our parents were frustrated, our friends were angry and jealous, our neighbors were sick of us, and our pets were feeling deprived and rejected because we had ignored them. Our old life had been abandoned for a new life, and we didn't care whether others thought we used our time wisely or even if they thought we were crazy. We were oblivious to the world around us. It didn't exist. We were children, and for a few short weeks we were allowed to abandon ourselves into the world of our imaginations.

I miss that summer very much. In all the years of my childhood, I was never as alive as I was during those weeks. Every day was vivid, electric, adventurous, invigorating, and exhilarating. Every nerve was standing on tiptoe, every sense was activated, every emotion was alive! My whole being was on call, on alert.

In the summer of 1952, in the unlikely sanctuary of refrigerator and washing machine boxes, I was given my first taste of abandon, my first experience of giving myself over unrestrainedly to an idea larger than myself. God was gifting me, preparing me for that moment when I would bump into Jesus and He would beckon me to come, abandon all else, and follow Him.

BEYOND CAREFULNESS

In the beginning of His ministry, Jesus was continually bumping into fishermen, tax collectors, and political activists and asking them to follow Him. Astonishingly, these men abandoned their careers, their families, and their futures to follow Jesus. All because this Jesus said, "Follow Me." Why? Why would these men give up all they knew to follow Jesus into what they didn't know? Because somehow these men *knew* that life with Jesus is the life they had been seeking unsuccessfully in the confines of safety and caution. They *knew* life's greatest adventure was waiting just beyond the limits of carefulness. They *knew* where the music was coming from.

Jesus said, "Whoever loses his life for My sake will find it." In modern language Jesus is saying whoever *abandons* his life will *live* life to its fullest. "Go for it! Taste the new wine of a life which defies the law of gravity, a life which throws caution to the wind, where danger and risk await!" Jesus is saying, "Abandon yourself to the One who will never abandon you."

Truth is, most of us have lost touch with the childlike experience of abandon. We believe in Jesus, we love the idea of Jesus, we try to do what we believe He wants us to do, but *abandon everything?* Abandon our job, our security, our nice home, our parents' expectations for us, our future? Sounds scary. To be quite honest, abandon sounds irresponsible and crazy.

Abandon *is* definitely unpredictable, a loose cannon that could go off at any time. We can't have people running around discarding responsible behavior in the name of Jesus. After all, every society has rules. Rules are the structures that protect us from anarchy. They tell us how we are to behave and what we are supposed to do and when we are supposed to do it. Rules and laws protect society from chaos and confusion. We can't have people breaking the rules in the name of Jesus, can we?

Unrule-ly Behavior

Let's look at children again.

Little children start their lives un*rule*-ly, without rules, oblivious to society's prescribed laws, which, according to the rule makers of our society, exist for children's and everyone's good. Eventually children are socialized. Domesticated. They *learn* how to behave, how to conform to the cultural "norms" for the greater good of society. Children are told that learning the rules, becoming responsible and orderly, and discovering the boundaries of a civilized world are what growing up is all about.

But is it?

Or, in the process of socializing our children to follow the rules, do we rob them of the discernment needed to know when to follow rules and when to break them? Have we robbed our children (including those of us who have grown out of childhood) of the childlike intuition that caused us to know in our hearts how to recognize *the Rule Maker?* Christianity is this wild religion that has always been more concerned about following Jesus than following the rules of Jesus.

Remember when you said yes to Jesus that first time? You didn't know all the rules, but you knew Jesus. Sadly, the church immediately stepped in and told us we needed to know more than Jesus; we needed to know the rules of the Christian faith, otherwise we might end up in confusion and spiritual anarchy. The church is always worried we might make a mistake!

Mistakes are the guaranteed consequence of wild abandon. Mistakes are signs of growth. That is why the Old and New Testament are full of people who made mistakes. The church should be the one place in our culture where mistakes are not only expected but welcomed.

Every time the disciples started establishing rules—no children near Jesus; don't let the crowd touch Jesus; don't talk to Samaritan women; don't let people waste expensive per-fumes—Jesus told them to knock it off, and His rebuke was usually followed by a lecture that said, "You still don't get it! We are not substituting religious rules with our rules. We are substituting religious rules with *Me!*" Jesus kept saying "Follow *Me*," not "follow My rules." So most of us have spent our Christian lives learning what we *can't* do instead of cele-brating what we *can* do in Jesus.

THE RULE BREAKER

What a tragedy. What a misunderstanding of who Jesus is. It was Jesus who taught us how to *break* the rules.

It was Jesus who touched lepers, *against the rules*. (No one was to touch a leper.)

It was Jesus who broke the Sabbath, *against the rules*. (The Pharisees had thousands of rules against working on the Sabbath.)

It was Jesus who forgave people of their sins, *against the rules*. (Adulterers were to be stoned, not forgiven.)

The religious leaders accused Jesus of breaking the rules over and over again. They made it very clear that Messiahs do not touch lepers, work on the Sabbath, forgive adulterers, and hang around with "sinners." Jesus made it very clear — *this Messiah* does *touch lepers and forgive adulterers. This Messiah is wild and serves His Father with abandon.* Jesus was the Rule Breaker because He is the Rule Maker. He alone decides what rules are true and what rules are nonsense. That is why we follow Christ with abandon wherever He takes us. *He* lets us know which rules are for following and which rules are for breaking.

Sounds alarming. Hazardous, even. Exactly! Faith is about recklessly following Jesus wherever He goes. (Notice I said wherever Jesus goes. Reckless abandon does not mean we make the rules and He follows us. Following Christ with abandon does not give us permission to kill those who make rules we don't agree with. Remember, Jesus let the rule monitors use their rules to kill Him.) Genuine faith is hazardous to your health. Better hang on and fasten your seat belt because following Jesus to the wherevers of life is much more precarious than most of us realize. Again, can you feel your pulse begin to quicken? Aren't you intrigued, just like a child, to find out more about this daring and treacherous faith?

In the book of John (6:25-66) Jesus was teaching His rule-breaking message in the synagogue in Capernaum. "I am the bread that came down from heaven," He said. Many of His followers were beginning to balk at what they were hearing. "Hey," they said. (This is a loose translation—very loose.) "This stuff You are talking about is *crazy*. You say You are from heaven, but we played with You as a kid. We know Your mom and dad. Last time we read the Old Testament, Messiahs don't play hide-and-seek! The rule makers say anyone who calls himself God is a blasphemer. You tell us You are bread and water and life, which is to claim You are God. The rule makers say people like You are the Devil." John tells us, "From this time many of his disciples turned back and no longer followed him" (verse 66).

No wonder. Jesus was too bizarre. Too radical. Too dangerous. He was breaking too many rules. If you follow a rule breaker, you do so at your own peril. No wonder everyone left Him. Or did they? Brace yourself. *Not all the disciples turned back!* Some of the disciples, including Peter, decided to stay with Jesus. Jesus Himself was surprised and questioned those who remained, *"You* aren't leaving Me?" Peter answered the question for himself and all of us: "Lord, to whom shall we go? You have the words of eternal life" (verse 68).

Peter was speaking from deep within himself. He was saying what he had yet to fully understand, echoing the very thoughts we all have had—there is nowhere else to go *except* to follow Jesus.

Peter uttered what we need to understand—real Christianity is more than wild abandon; it is about abandon*ing:*

- The rich young ruler could not abandon his riches.
- The Pharisees could not abandon their religion.
- Pilate could not abandon his power.

What is it you and I are afraid to abandon? Our comfort? Our schedules? Our careers? Our money? Our possessions? Our security? Our theology? Our need for certainty? Our fear of making a mistake? Our parents' expectations?

If only the rich young ruler had abandoned his riches, he could have discovered the richness of following Jesus.

If only the Pharisees could have abandoned their rules, they could have spent every day basking in the love of the Rule Maker.

If only Pilate could have abandoned his power, he would have found the real power of brokenness and humility.

So what do you say? Let's become like children again, break away from the rule keepers, and make a run for Jesus.

A LIFE OF ABANDON

Sounds good, doesn't it? Except for one problem—our fear. We are afraid to follow Christ with abandon.

We were spending a few days with family when our grandson Noah, fifteen-months-old at the time, noticed the hot tub at the hotel. Instantly he broke loose from our grasp, ran to the edge of the hot tub, squealing excitedly, "Wah-wah!" Faster than our minds could have predicted, he stood at the edge of the tub, ready to jump. No fear. None. Luckily, we were able to stop him before it occurred to him that it is impossible to breathe under water. At fifteen months, Noah's rule of life was "Jump first, fear later." It would take a few more months for Noah to learn a rule of life we've all learned: "Fear first, jump later."

Granted, in the case of the hot tub, fear is an effective deterrent from drowning, but, sadly, as he grows older his fear could easily keep him from jumping into the water again. For many of us, the fear that protected us from dying when we were young prohibits us from living now. Fear keeps us from experimenting, from taking chances, from trying the new, from choosing the discomfort of exploring uncharted waters, from stepping out in the darkness, from going where no one else has gone.

Jesus was continually saying to those around Him, "Don't be afraid." He understood that in this world no one is safe. We all take risks every day—the issue is, what risks we are willing to take. Following Jesus is risky. He told His disciples in

Matthew 10, "If you come after Me, nothing you own is safe, including *you*." When we follow the rule-violating, religion-threatening, category-breaking Jesus, our lives are always in jeopardy.

The Christian life is more than finding Jesus—it is *following* Jesus. Following, it turns out, is not a one-time, spectacular act of faith, but a one-day-at-a-time, ordinary, unspectacular following; a daily act of fearlessness that takes us through the most frightening and rugged terrain to a place of peace, joy, and abandon.

Those who follow Christ with abandon are quietly fearless. They face the most difficult circumstances with determination and constancy regardless of whether they receive recognition or encouragement.

It's the "reckless" abandon of the mother who rejects the advice of doctors and family who tell her to abort her Down's syndrome child, who every day thereafter cares for her daughter and sees Jesus smiling each night as she surrenders in exhaustion to a very long day, only to discover in the morning just enough strength to make it through another day.

It's the wild abandon of a dentist who gives up his lucrative practice to care for his wife with Alzheimer's when everyone, including his children, believes he is making a terrible mistake, only to find—in the tiny instants of her partial recognition and the final squeeze of his hand as she dies—Jesus' tears of admiration and love.

It's the irresponsible abandon of a young woman who leaves a brilliant career in television to work in the hopelessly poor villages of Brazil, making a home for street kids who have been abandoned by their families.[3] As she falls asleep exhausted, she hears the gentle lullaby of Jesus' approval.

It's the determined abandon of the helper at a L'Arche community who tenderly cares for a twenty-five-year-old man whose limbs sprawl haphazardly from his body, purposeless, lost, not knowing which direction to go, as though seized by some alien force. Yet, every day, twenty-four long hours a day, this man's anonymous helper holds him, bathes him, becomes his arms and legs, translates the voice imprisoned inside this body. The cost is high, the demands endless, the burnout rate almost 100 percent after two years, and yet, as his helper packs his bags and says goodby . . . the man cries. Somehow this impossibly wired being unscrambles the tangle of his body's conflicting messages, breaks the code, and wills his body to produce a tear. A miracle, really. A tribute to the wild abandon of someone who has followed Jesus to this place and now hears Him say, through the tear of His broken child, "Thank you. Thank you."

Actually, the Bible is filled with stories of people characterized by wild abandon.

The woman with a humiliating blood disease who braved the ridicule and anger of the crowd with abandon so she could reach Jesus and touch Him (Mark 5:25-34). The abandon of a widow who came every day to the temple to give her small offering in the face of enormous ridicule from a culture that demeaned the size of her gift (Luke 21:1-4).

A life of abandon is a life of resistance, a lonely life, a minority life, and, above all, an incomprehensible life.

Last year Bill Harley, singer, songwriter, and storyteller, told a marvelous story on National Public Radio's *All Things Considered*. It is the story of a young girl who ended up breaking the rules, rejecting the expectations of all around her, because she loved with abandon. Here is her story:

> Last year, my young son played T-ball. . . . Needless to
> say, I was delighted when Dylan wanted to play. . . .
> Now on the other team there was a girl I will call Tracy.
> Tracy came each week. I know, since my son's team
> always played her team. She was not very good. She
> had coke-bottle glasses and hearing aids on each ear.
> She ran in a loping, carefree way, with one leg pulling
> after the other, one arm windmilling wildly in the air.
> Everyone in the bleachers cheered for her, regard-

less of what team their progeny played for. In all the games I saw, she never hit the ball, not even close. It sat there on the tee waiting to be hit and it never was. Sometimes, after ten or eleven swings, Tracy hit the tee (in T-ball, the ball sits on a plastic tee, waiting for the batter to hit the ball, which happens once every three batters). The ball would fall off the tee and sit on the ground six inches in front of home plate. "Run! Run!" yelled Tracy's coach, and Tracy would lope off to first, clutching the bat in both arms, smiling. Someone usually woke up and ran her down with the ball before she reached first.

Everyone applauded.

The last game of the season, Tracy came up, and through some fluke, or simply in a nod toward the law of averages, she creamed the ball. She smoked it right up the middle, through the legs of 17 players. Kids dodged as it went by or looked absentmindedly at it as it rolled unstopped, seemingly gaining in speed, hopping over second base, heading into center field. And once it reached there, there was no one to stop it. Have I told you that there are no outfielders in T-ball? There are for three minutes in the beginning of every inning, but then they move into the infield to be closer to the action, or, at least, to their friends.

Tracy hit the ball and stood at home, delighted. "Run!" yelled her coach. "Run!" All the parents, all of us, we stood and screamed, "Run, Tracy, run, run!" Tracy turned and smiled at us, and then, happy to please, galumphed off to first. The first base coach waved his arms 'round and 'round when Tracy stopped at first. "Keep going, Tracy, keep going! Go!" Happy to please, she headed to second. By the time she was halfway to second, seven members of the opposition had reached the ball and were passing it among themselves. It's a rule in T-ball—everyone on the defending team has to touch every ball.

The ball began to make its long and circuitous route toward home plate, passing from one side of the field to the other. Tracy headed to third. Adults fell out of the bleachers. "Go, Tracy, go!" Tracy reached third and stopped, but the parents were very close to her now and she got the message. Her coach stood at home plate calling her as the ball passed over the first baseman's head and landed in the fielding team's empty dugout. "Come on, Tracy! Come on, baby! Get a home run!"

Tracy started for home, and then it happened. During the pandemonium, no one had noticed the twelve-year-old geriatric mutt that had lazily settled itself down in front of the bleachers five feet from the third-base line. As Tracy rounded third, the dog, awakened by the screaming, sat up and wagged its tail at Tracy as she headed down the line. The tongue hung out, mouth pulled back in an unmistakable canine smile, and Tracy stopped, right there. Halfway home, thirty feet from a legitimate home run.

She looked at the dog. Her coach called, "Come on, Tracy! Come on home!" He went to his knees behind the plate, pleading. The crowd cheered, "Go, Tracy, go! Go Tracy, go!" She looked at all the adults, at her own parents shrieking and catching it all on video. She looked at the dog. The dog wagged its tail. She looked at her coach. She looked at home. She looked at the dog. Everything went to slow motion. She went for the dog! It was a moment of complete, stunned silence. And then, perhaps, not as loud, but deeper, longer, more heartfelt, we all applauded as Tracy fell to her knees to hug the dog. Two roads diverged on a third-base line. Tracy went for the dog.[4]

Two roads diverged in this little girl's life. One is the road of rules and expectations, the other is the road of love. The roads of our lives are much the same. Will we go for the safe, predictable road of rules and expectations? Or will we go for the One we love, Jesus, who bids us come with wild abandon?

CHAPTER FOUR

Daring Playfulness

Life is tough. It takes up much of your time,
all your weekends, and what do you get in the end of it? I
think that the life cycle is all backward.
You should die first, get that out of the way. Then you live
twenty years in an old-age home. You get kicked out when
you're too young. You get a gold watch, you go to work.
You work forty years until you're young enough to enjoy
your retirement. You go to college; you party until you're
ready for high school; you go to grade school; you become a
little kid; you play. You have no responsibilities.
You become a little baby; you go back into the womb;
you spend your last nine months floating; and you finish
up as a gleam in somebody's eye.[1]

I was never young because
I never dared to be young.[2]

IT WAS A NORMAL WEEKEND FOR A NINE-YEAR-OLD. LIKE MOST children in the 1950s, I was subject to a bedtime which had been extended thirty minutes because of summer vacation. An only child, I often invited friends over for the weekend. One rainy Saturday night, my friend and I decided to make my bedroom an imaginary cave. We pretended to be lost in our completely dark cave with no hope of getting out.

Our "cave" was my bed covered with blankets so that no light could creep under the bed where our two sleeping bags lay. To make the cave environment more treacherous, we surrounded the bed with a web of chairs, pillows, and lamps, complete with a secret entrance constructed from coat hangers and towels. We had to be very quiet so that my father didn't hear us. (My Italian father believed bedtime was bedtime. Period.) After carefully and quietly building our cave, we both crawled under the bed, where we planned to remain "trapped" for the remainder of the evening. Soon, however, we decided to make our escape.

We began our journey out of the cave quietly, carefully working our way through the maze. The goal was to make it without being detected (by my father) to the top of the cave (bed), where we would be free. After a close call when one of our lamps fell over, we made it to the top of the bed and began bouncing, when suddenly, we became aware of a law of physics. We noticed that if one of us timed his jump so that he landed from his leap at the split second the other person was pushing off the bed, he would go much higher on his jump, and consequently, upon landing would propel his partner to even greater heights. We both realized at the same time that with practice we might be able to touch the ceiling. There was no question what we had to do—we had to touch the ceiling! It was our destiny!

The more we bounced, the more determined we became, and the more oblivious we were to the thunderous noise our bed was making every time one of us landed.

Suddenly the door to my bedroom swung open and the huge shadow of my father fell across the room, his body silhouetted in the hallway like some prehistoric monster. His voice could be heard two houses down: "GET IN BED *NOW!*" We must have looked like frozen Gumbies, waiting for the bouncing to stop. Neither of us said a word. Both of us forgot about the cave, slowly slid the extra blankets off the bed, and crawled under the covers. My father shut the door and we went to sleep.

My father is a good and loving man; he was just doing what all fathers would do when it sounds like an earthquake is going on in their sons' room. But as I look back over the forty-six years since that night, I am struck with an odd awareness. *I never bounced on my bed again.*

If you can't bounce on your bed at nine years old, when can you? Before you know it, you not only stop bouncing on your bed, you stop skipping, you stop playing hide-and-seek, you stop *playing!*

"MOVE OVER, GUYS, I'LL SHOW YOU BOUNCING!"

I often wonder what would have happened that night if Jesus would have opened the door and caught us jumping on the bed. There is no way to know, of course, but my guess is that Jesus might have looked at us for a moment, laughed, and said, "Move over, guys, I'll show you bouncing!"

For over twenty years Craig McNair Wilson, a one-man drama troupe, performed a two-hour drama of the life of Christ called *The Fifth Gospel*. How he did it is still a mystery, but Craig would be all the characters—the disciples, Jesus, Pilate, the leper, the blind man, and so forth. He loved to reenact the disciples and Jesus taking a break in the river Jordan.

Jesus and the disciples were all in the river taking baths

when the beloved disciple, John, reaches down to the floor of the river and brings up a huge mud pie. Preoccupied with their washing, none of the disciples notices. John takes careful aim at his favorite target, Peter. *SPLAT!* The mud pie strikes Peter in the face. John immediately ducks underwater as though he is scrubbing. Peter reaches for his own mud pie, takes careful aim at Matthew, and lets it fly. *WHAM!* James wastes no time responding with his own mud pie, and soon bedlam breaks out amongst the disciples. A full-fledged mud fight is under way. Philip and Bartholomew sneak up on Judas, whom they didn't particularly like anyway, and nail him with two mud pies. Simon the Zealot, who has never been particularly close to John because he thinks he's a wimp, lets loose with a huge mud pie. John ducks and the mud missile hits Jesus right in the middle of His forehead. All the disciples freeze. After a long silence Thomas leans over to Simon and says, "You idiot! You just hit the Son of God with a mud pie. . . . He'll turn us into turtles!" Jesus gazes slowly at each of the disciples, each one fearing the worst. With a knowing smile, Jesus stops when He sees Simon, who refuses to look in Jesus' eyes. Jesus reaches down into the mud and comes up with a very large mud pie and — *BAM!* — Simon is hit squarely on the top of his head, and as the mud slithers down his face, everyone, including Jesus, breaks into laughter.

Craig McNair Wilson understands the nature of Jesus as I understand it. Jesus Christ knew how to play as well as pray; how to laugh as well as cry; how to be serious about life but not take Himself too seriously. Jesus Christ came to save us from our sin and to save us from becoming severe, unyielding, harsh, and terminally serious. One cannot read the Sermon on the Mount without getting a hint of the playfulness of Jesus:

- His remarks about fasting — "Do not look somber as the hypocrites do." (Matthew 6:16)
- His comments about worrying — "Look at the birds of the air; they do not sow or reap or store away in barns, and yet your heavenly Father feeds them. Are

you not much more valuable than they? Who of you by worrying can add a single hour to his life? . . . See how the lilies of the field grow. They do not labor or spin." (Matthew 6:26-28)

- His remarks about prayer — "Which of you, if his son asks for bread, will give him a stone? Of if he asks for a fish, will give him a snake?" (Matthew 7:9-10)
- His remarks about the wise and foolish builders — "But everyone who hears these words of mine and does not put them into practice is like a foolish man who built his house on sand." (Matthew 7:26)

Jesus' words are filled with playfulness, irony, metaphor, and hyperbole. He must have said them with a twinkle in His eye. He continuously used stories, parables, and actual events to expose the blindness of His critics. When the stakes were high, when men and women's souls were hanging in the balance, when truth was on the line, Jesus would *play* with His listeners, would verbally spar with His critics, forcing into the open those who cared nothing about truth. No wonder that when Jesus was done speaking, "the crowds were amazed at his teaching" (Matthew 7:28). No wonder people said, "He taught as one who had authority, and *not as their teachers of the law*" (Matthew 7:29, emphasis added). Jesus' words were not somber, oppressive, smothering, and threatening; they were lively, full of colorful images and earthy characters — fun stories that left His listeners wanting more.

In *Living the Message* Eugene Peterson points out how powerful a playful parable can be:

Jesus' favorite speech form, the parable, was subversive. Parables sound absolutely ordinary: casual stories about soil and seeds, meals and coins and sheep, bandits and victims, farmers and merchants. And they are wholly secular: of his forty or so parables recorded in the Gospels, only one has its setting in church, and

only a couple mention the name God. As people heard
Jesus tell these stories, they saw at once that they
weren't about God, so there was nothing in them
threatening their own sovereignty. They relaxed their
defenses. They walked away perplexed, wondering
what they meant, the stories lodged in their imagination. And then, like a time bomb, they would explode
in their unprotected hearts. An abyss opened up at
their very feet. He *was* talking about God; they had
been invaded![3]

Jesus understood He could protect the seriousness of the
gospel by interspersing His life and message with a sense of
playfulness.

IS PLAY FRIVOLOUS?

When people hear that I pastor a church, they immediately
communicate their discomfort. They don't know how to act in
the presence of a minister and assume that frivolity and play
are not appropriate.

Two teenage boys, who know I'm a minister, live next
door to us, and they had kept their distance, seldom waving
or acknowledging me when we bumped into each other—
until a recent night in July. My wife and I were sitting out on
the deck of our home around ten o'clock. The two boys were
playing basketball on their driveway with some friends. The
friends had parked their truck on the lawn, opened up the
doors, and turned up the music to full volume. Without parents to contend with, their basketball game was loud and bois-
terous. Boys ought to be playing basketball on a hot summer
night, but I decided to add a little life to the evening.

"July Fourth was two weeks ago," I mentioned to my wife.

"That's good, honey," she said. "Glad to see you are in the
same month as the rest of us."

"No, no. I mean I have a few fireworks left over, and I feel like having some fun with the boys next door. Let's throw a couple of firecrackers over the fence and see what happens."

She looked at me sternly. "Are you serious?"

"Yes," I said mischievously.

"OKAY!" she said. "Let's go!"

Our adventure began with my wife standing behind a tree while I walked along the fence until I thought I was close enough. I threw a firecracker over the wall, ran back to the tree where my wife was, and waited. Nothing. The boys couldn't hear anything because the music and the game were too loud. Undaunted, I crept closer this time, with a *string* of firecrackers, and lobbed them over the fence. Bang! *Bang-bang-bang-bang-bang!*

The music stopped, the lights went out, and the boys all yelled, "What was that?" Then they all ran into the house and returned a few minutes later, each brandishing a flashlight. We could hear them speculating on who the perpetrator was. "It must have been Jessica [our daughter]. No, maybe it was Jonathan [the *other* next-door neighbor]." Flashlights were bobbing as the boys headed to the fence to search the other side. My wife and I were hiding behind a tree a long way from the search area when, without warning, a boy with a huge flashlight jumped up from behind the fence and caught us by surprise. The look on his face was incredible. He stared at us for a few seconds, assimilating what he was seeing, and then yelled to the others, "Oh my gosh! It's the parents!" Ten minutes later our house was covered with toilet paper. We responded with water balloons.

My relationship with the neighbor boys has never been the same. When we bump into each other, we laugh, joke, and find conversation easy. The minister stereotype has been broken, and now we are friends because of some childlike playfulness.

Just because we believe the gospel is a life-and-death matter doesn't mean we have to act as if we're dead. Apparently people knew how to be playful even in Jesus' time. Certainly being paralyzed is a serious matter. But in the second chapter of Mark, verses 1-12, we find a most delightful incident in the life of Christ. Jesus had begun to attract a crowd, a *large crowd*. He was in a home teaching when the crowd became so large that "there was no room left, not even outside the door" (verse 2).

A group of men had brought a paralytic to Jesus, and because there was no way to get to Him, they decided to carry the man to the roof of the house and rip it open. Think about the outrageousness of their behavior. They were tearing apart someone else's roof to get close to Jesus. I can see them gleefully tearing the roof apart amidst loud criticism suggesting that such behavior was immature at best. But they didn't care. They were having the time of their lives, and besides, the roof could be repaired later. Immature, silly, irresponsible (there's that word again!). Jesus, however, honored their behavior. He was impressed with the men's faith, not concerned about their "immaturity," and appreciated their ingenuity. No lectures. No rebuke. I believe He honored the friends' playful inventiveness when He healed the paralytic.

Time for a reality check, right? Playfulness is not a welcome idea for most of us. It sounds frivolous and shallow, distracting and irrelevant, inefficient and unproductive. That's because we live in a technological culture that worships busyness and activity. Under the guise of saving time, we now are inundated with e-mail, pagers, and cellular phones. We end each day smothered by the demands of our time and are greeted each new morn with more to do, not less. Play? There's no time to play. How can we play when the mountain of work and problems we are faced with each day get higher and deeper? How can we play when the world is overcome with poverty, famine, and war?

Play is an expression of God's presence in the world; one clear sign of God's absence in society is the absence of playfulness and laughter. Play is not an escape; it is the way to release the life-smothering grip of busyness, stress, and anxiety. (Playfulness is a modern expression of hope, a celebration of the flickering light of the gospel that plays with the dark by pouncing on the surrounding darkness like a cat toying with a mouse.)

A PLAYFUL RESPONSE

Instead of Christians wearing sackcloth and ashes at the condition of our world, maybe we should strike up a game of capture the flag in our neighborhood. Our neighbors may need Jesus, but first they need a rousing evening of charades. Certainly our children need discipline, but what they may need more is a family Ping-Pong championship. What if our strategy to win the world was to "play" people into the kingdom of God? What if we invited people over to our home and, instead of telling them about our joy, lived it by playing with them? What if we could hear laughter in a church as well as "amens"? A friend of mine is a member of a church who toyed with making their motto "The Church That Knows How to Play." I think he's onto something.

What if the family became a place that played together as well as prayed together?

Seventeen years is a long time to know someone, and Ron's parents thought they knew him. What had happened during the previous summer, though, Ron's parents had no idea. All they knew was that when school began, their "normal," straight-A son had become a "punker." Black was the only color he would wear—a black Metallica T-shirt, black pants, black motorcycle boots—and with his earring-adorned, shaved head (seven earrings total) and his nonstop obsession with heavy metal music, the seventeen-year-old Ron showed very little resemblance to the sixteen-year-old version. Mom and Dad were worried. Home had become a war zone. Each day when they came home from work they'd have to storm downstairs to Ron's locked bedroom where the music was so loud the walls were shaking. They would bang on the door and loudly ask Ron to turn down the music.

After six months of escalating tension, Ron's parents decided to get counseling before they lost their child. Many issues came to the surface and the process went on for many months, but one of the solutions the counselor suggested sounded so bizarre they were reluctant to try it. "When you both get home tonight," he advised, "go down to your son's room, bang on the door, and when he answers tell him to turn his music off and come upstairs because you both want to talk to him. When he finally saunters into the room with a chip on his shoulder and slumps into the kitchen chair with an attitude, look him square in the eyes and say, 'Ron, your mother and I are counting to one hundred. Now go hide.'"

When you love your son like these parents did, desperation combined with love will motivate you to try anything—even play. And one night that is what they did. Can you imagine the look on Ron's face? Can you imagine what Ron said to his friends the next day? "You guys are never going to guess what happened last night. I played hide-and-seek with my parents until three in the morning. I still can't find them." Ron didn't become a Republican or start listening to country and western music, but when his parents played hide-and-seek with him, they did break through the longstanding tension and began the long process of healing.

A family I know was facing a very difficult financial crisis. Finances were so bad that the parents were on the verge of losing their business and, with Christmas coming, things were looking very bleak. Providing enough food and clothes for the family was difficult, and Christmas gifts were out of the question. Mom and Dad decided to tell their five children the truth about their situation. They would not be able to afford Christmas presents this year, and they requested help in deciding what to do about it. The children responded excitedly, "Let's have a coupon Christmas. Instead of giving each other presents that cost money, let's give each other coupons worth some kind of service." And that year each person in the family received a book of coupons with the following gifts:

From the kids to one another:

> When you don't want to do the dishes, present this coupon and I will do the dishes for you without complaining.*
>
> *Good ONE time only.

> Behind on your laundry? No problem. Present this coupon to me and I will gladly do your laundry.*
>
> *Good ONE time only.

And from the parents:

> Anti-grounding certificate. Keep this until Mom and I have forgotten we gave it to you. When you are grounded for whatever reason, present this coupon and you will be forgiven the grounding.*
>
> *Definitely good ONE time only.

Every member of the family unequivocally states to this day that the best Christmas they ever had was the "Coupon Christmas."

In this family's playfulness, they discovered that God was hiding in the "poverty" of their financial situation.

GOD HIDES

The nature of God is playful, that is why He *hides*. God is not only present when we can see Him, He is present when we can't, and joy comes from recognizing God in places we never thought He would be. God hides in difficulty, He hides in suffering, He hides in poverty, He hides in failure, and He hides in the stories of our lives. Whatever our circumstance, whatever the status of our lives, God is present — invisible, hiding, waiting for us to discover Him, waiting for us to learn from Him in the shadows as well as the light.

I have already mentioned how life altering my experience at L'Arche was. So many of my expectations were shattered that week. I had expected to meet God in the lives of those who were "whole." Instead, God was hiding in the lives of the "broken," the mentally and physically challenged — especially in a girl I'll call Deborah. Her twenty-five-year-old body is ravaged by cerebral palsy and is as cooperative as a limp rag doll. She had to be held by someone at all times. Unable to speak, unable to respond, I wondered (I am embarrassed to admit now) why Henri had included her in our daily Bible studies.

I found out very soon. Two days after we arrived, Deborah was to celebrate her first Communion. It was a festive occasion and we were invited. We arrived at one of the L'Arche homes that was filled with sixty mentally and physically challenged members of the community, two dozen workers, and our study group. I had come with the expectation that this could be a great experience in the presence of God. Deborah was in a fully restrained wheelchair, her face radiant, her hair beautifully done, her dress stunning. The room was crowded and noisy and, as the Eucharist began, my heart sunk in disappointment.

The noise was chaotic and distracting. Those with Down's syndrome were humming loudly, continually, rocking back and forth to a rhythm only they could hear. One girl would suddenly let loose with an ear-piercing shriek every few seconds, and the service had to be stopped temporarily because one member of the community had an epileptic seizure. I was completely distracted, disappointed at the chaos and confusion that had ruined my experience with God. As Father Nouwen presented the body and blood of Christ to each person in the room, I was secretly pouting, secretly counting the minutes until I could leave.

When Father Nouwen stopped in front of Deborah, her body stopped jerking and moving out of control, her eyes glistened, she opened her mouth to receive the wine and the bread, and there, ever so slightly, I saw her smile! At once the noise in the room was transformed into what I imagined the noise at the nativity would have been like. *God was there!* His fragrance filled the room. Deborah—the girl who could do nothing, the girl who would never give a talk, the girl who would never dance, the girl who would never write a book or play the piano or sing a song—taught me about the grace of God! For fifty years I had struggled with God's unconditional love for me; for fifty years I had tried to prove my worthiness to God by busyness; and helpless Deborah might as well have grabbed me by the shoulders and shouted in my face, "God loves you just as you are! Surrender to His love!" I realized God was hiding in Deborah, and I haven't been the same since.

GOD HIDES *AND* SEEKS

But God does more than hide—He also seeks. Early one morning I was writing about faith. My office was a mess with reference books strewn over the entire surface of my desk, my couch, and my floor. After about two hours I began to sense the presence of God in my study. It was a very unusual experience for me but, at the same time, very real. It was as though He was playing with me. I went to the computer and wrote down my experience as it was happening.

> I sit in my room this morning, playing hide and seek with God, enjoying the seeking as much as the finding. Catching glimpses of my Father smiling, darting from one book to another, hiding in my mind. Suddenly He is standing there in my thoughts laughing, escaping my grasp, only to turn up on the page of my notes. As I gather my notes, my Bible, my books to prepare this talk, I find my soul overflowing with gratitude, with

the tears of joy because God and I have just spent two hours together, just He and I playing with truth, and I leave my study with a strange understanding that I did not find God . . . God found me.

God *does* play with our souls. He hides and He seeks and His laughter heals our hearts. When God plays with us, before we know it, we are playing: playing with our neighbors, our church members, and even our families.

WOULD YOU LIKE TO BUILD A SAND CASTLE?

Six years ago our family spent the weekend together on the Oregon coast. On Saturday all eight of us decided to spend the afternoon walking along the water. During our walk my oldest son, who was twenty-five at the time, ran up to me and said excitedly, "Let's build a sand castle." It must have been twenty years since either my wife or I had built a sand castle. Now *we* were excited. Our other son, then twenty-three, tied his T-shirt to a pole and stuck it just behind where we were to build the castle. He then set the challenge: "We must build a sand castle strong enough to keep the incoming water from knocking down the flag. If the flag hits the sand, then it turns to poison and we're all dead." We all accepted the challenge.

We were actively building a three-walled sand castle when I happened to look up and see a man walking down the beach with his son who looked to be about five years old. I thought, *How can we build a sand castle without a little boy?* Without thinking further, I left the building site, ran over to the boy, fell down on my knees, and pleaded, "Little boy, we need your help desperately. See that flag down there? We have to build a sand castle strong enough to keep the water from knocking down the flag or the sand is poison and we're all dead." You should have seen the look on the little boy's face. He looked up at his father as if he was thinking, *Dad, you warned me about people like this. Let's get out of here.* Neither the boy nor his father acknowledged my request, and they kept on walking down the beach.

After I had returned to our sand castle, I caught a glimpse of the little boy again. His dad let him run to the edge of the water, and he was playing tag with the waves. He would follow the water out and then run as it chased him up the beach. Unfortunately, he misjudged the waves and was knocked down by a surprise breaker. His father yelled, "Andy, get out of the water now." Andy, of course, was trying to do just that when I ran over to help him. I don't know what overcame me, but I found myself saying, "Andy, you are already wet and muddy. You might as well come help us." He looked at his father, then at me, and then back at his father. Finally, he said, "Okay!"

We were all working desperately because the tide was coming in, when one of the kids yelled, "Look out!" Instinctively, without anyone saying a word, we all bunched around the flag, eight of us in a group hug as the water washed over the first wall, smashed down the second wall, and rolled over the third wall—but the flag remained standing. We all let out a yell, including Andy. It was a great moment, and we all felt like kids again.

In the book of Matthew we are given a quick glimpse of the evangelist's life-changing meeting with Jesus. "As Jesus went on from there, he saw a man named Matthew sitting at the tax collector's booth. 'Follow me,' he told him, and Matthew got up and followed him" (Matthew 9:9).

No one knows what was going on in Matthew's mind when Jesus came up to him, but I have fantasized Jesus leaning over and whispering in his ear, "Hey, Matthew, want to build a sand castle?" I believe Matthew's heart almost leaped out of his skin, and he ended up following Jesus the rest of his life . . . wherever He went . . . to the beach, to the playground, and even to the cross.

CHAPTER FIVE

Wide-eyed Listening

A four-year-old girl was overheard whispering into her newborn baby brother's ear, "Baby," she whispers, "tell me what God sounds like. I am starting to forget."[1]

SADLY, BY THE TIME WE ARE ADULTS, MOST OF US HAVE LOST OUR God hearing. By the time we are adults, we have decided that listening *to* God is less important than knowing *about* God. By the time we are grown, we have jobs and children; the noise of our lives has increased to such a level that we couldn't possibly hear God because God rarely shouts—He whispers.

First Kings 19 contains the story of Elijah. After a hugely successful confrontation with the prophets of Baal, Elijah suddenly went into severe depression and ran into the desert to hide. When God confronted him, Elijah *pouted*. Isn't it great news that prophets pout? *I can do that!* God sent Elijah to Mount Horeb where He produced a "great and powerful wind [which] tore the mountains apart and shattered the rocks" (verse 11). Then He sent an earthquake and a fire. After the fire, the Bible tells us in verse 12, depending on which translation you read, God spoke in "a still small voice" (KJV), "a gentle whisper" (NIV and TLB), "a sound of a gentle blowing" (NASB), "a sound of sheer silence" (NRSV), or "a light murmuring sound" (NJB).

A friend of mine, a Lutheran missionary to Africa, translates the passage, "a thin silence." *A thin silence!* Wow! God wasn't heard in the noise of the earthquake, the wind, and the fire; God was in the *thin silence.* Could it be that one of the significant problems in the church is noise? Modern faith might be undermined more by activity and noise than by immorality and lack of commitment. Maybe we have become so active and noisy that we have drowned out the thin silence of God. What if we decided to be kids again, to learn again how to listen to the voice of God? Instead of our trying to do *more*, maybe we should try to do *less*, to *pay attention* to the presence of God.

HEARING THE THIN SILENCE OF GOD

In *Stories Jesus Still Tells,* John Claypool relates the story of his daughter, Laura, who eventually died of leukemia. When she was four, John was attempting to put her to bed one night, but she was like most four-year-olds. To avoid going to bed, Laura took three trips to the bathroom, asked for a drink of water, wanted another story told, needed Dad to put the light on, heard a sound, and so on. John finally took care of his daughter's needs and went upstairs to write. He was deep into his writing when (if you have children, you know this experience) he could tell Laura was standing at the door of his study, staring at him. He hadn't seen her or heard anything, he just knew.

Frustrated, he turned around and said, with a bit of anger in his voice, "What do you want me to do, Laura?" Laura sauntered up beside her father, grabbed his arm, and said, "Nothing, Daddy, I just want to be close to you."[2]

Laura may have been speaking the words of God to us: "I don't want you to do anything. I just want to be next to you." I wonder how many times a day our Father tries to get our attention, tries to quiet us long enough so we can hear His whisper.

Our church recently held a one-day retreat for adults. A couple of the young people decided they wanted to attend as well. We spent the day reading different Scriptures, meditating on the Scripture and then journaling an assigned task. All participants were asked to journal, individually, what they thought Jesus might say to them if He wrote them a letter. When we gathered as a group to read our journal entries, the adults found it difficult to read theirs. Many were so concerned about interpreting Scripture correctly that they were afraid to be embarrassed by their lack of understanding. Janie, a seventeen-year-old high school girl, volunteered to read hers first. "First of all," she said hesitantly, "I think I messed up. You wanted us to write about what Jesus would

say to us, and instead, I wrote a dialogue between Jesus and
me." (Interesting, isn't it? Her first concern was that she
messed up, which is why children lose their ability to listen
to God.) We assured her that whatever she had written was
fine. Here is her dialogue:

i feel awkward
because it's been so long
since i've been near you.
> i've missed you too;
> i think about you every day.
But i've messed up;
i've done a lot of things
that i regret.
> it's okay, child.
> i forgive you.
i don't understand
i turn away,
i ignore you . . .
> i'm still here
> right beside you.
i try to live without you
even though i know deep inside
that you're still a part of me.
> you don't have to make yourself lovable;
> i love you how you are.
even after everything i've done,
and everything that has happened,
would it offend you if i called you bizarre?
> i am bizarre;
> more so than you'll ever know.
this may seem strange,
but could i please ask you
to hold me, for a little while?
> my child, i've been waiting for you
> with outstretched arms.[3]

After Janie read her dialogue, there wasn't a dry eye in the place . . . and all the adults said, "I'm not reading mine." Janie was still able to hear the "thin silence" of God.

Christianity isn't so complicated, is it? All we need to do is listen to the whisper of God.

We can find our hearing again. We can learn once again to hear the thin silence of God.

If we don't understand God as the Whisperer, the Thin Silence, then maybe we need to look at God in a new way. Maybe we need to abandon our "sophisticated" adult ways of understanding God and remember what we knew about God as a child.

IMPERSONATING OURSELVES

In *All I Really Need to Know I Learned in Kindergarten*, Robert Fulghum tells of the day he was left with eighty boys and girls, all five years old. It was his job to keep these children occupied for one hour, a seemingly impossible task. In desperation he remembered the game "Giants, Wizards, and Dwarfs," which is similar to "Rock, Paper, Scissors." It required each child, on command, to pair with another child and act out being a giant, a wizard, or a dwarf. The giant beat the wizard, the wizard beat the dwarf, and the dwarf beat the giant. Fulghum let the children run around for a few minutes to wear them out, and then he yelled, "Giants, Wizards, and Dwarfs!!" Organized chaos ensued as the children each found a partner, began acting out either a giant, a wizard, or a dwarf, and then tried to decide who won.

While this noisy mayhem was in progress, Fulghum felt a tug on his pant leg. He looked down to see a five-year-old girl with huge blue eyes looking up at him. "Yes," he said.

The little girl replied, "Um, where do the mermaids go?" Even though Fulghum had made it clear there were only three categories in this game, the little girl was not deterred. She was saying in unmistakable terms, "You may believe that only giants, wizards, and dwarfs exist, Mr. Fulghum, but you are wrong! *I* am a mermaid! Deal with it."[4]

I admire the little girl. She refused to accept that the categories given to choose from were the only ones. She understood her calling. She knew who she was.

Eugene Peterson pointed out once that most of us spend our lives "impersonating ourselves."[5] Children are who they are. It doesn't take long before we have convinced them that they are what they wear, or what they do, or what they have, or what they look like. But, if our children are lucky, we convince them early on to resist caricature or illusion. Once we decide, no matter how early in our lives, to quit listening to the way we are made, we begin to lose our God hearing. As Jeremiah understood, God started speaking to us in the womb.

> "Before I formed you in the womb I knew you,
>> before you were born I set you apart." (Jeremiah 1:5)

The moment we deny God's fingerprint on our soul, the instant we stop listening to our uniqueness, our God hearing starts to deteriorate. Jeremiah found that out. Being a prophet wasn't fun anymore. He was angry with God's call to be a prophet. He no longer wanted to make prophetic utterances, so he decided to stop talking, to deny his calling, and this is what happened:

> But if I say, "I will not mention him
>> or speak any more in his name,"
> *his word is in my heart like a fire,*
>> *a fire shut up in my bones.*
> I am weary of holding it in;
>> indeed, I cannot. (Jeremiah 20:9, emphasis added)

Jeremiah discovered that to deny the way he was made was to deny "his word," God's voice, God's whispering presence in his life. Jeremiah wrestled all his life with the truth that

God's calling is God *calling*. To turn our back on His calling voice is the beginning of deafness. The way to begin to hear God's word speaking to us is to pay attention to how God has shaped us. In the movie *Chariots of Fire*, when Eric Liddell, the Olympic runner, was challenged by his sister to forget the Olympics and go straight to the mission field, he replied, "Ah, but, darlin', I can run. And when I run, *I feel God's pleasure.*" He could not turn from his calling, from the way he was made.

GOD IS CHASING US

In Margaret Wise Brown's classic children's story *The Runaway Bunny*, the bunny announces to his mother that he is running away, and the mother responds, "If you run away, then I will run after you. For you are my little bunny." The bunny runs everywhere, but the mother keeps running after him until finally, at the end of the book, the little bunny realizes his predicament. "Shucks," he says, "I might just as well stay where I am and be your little bunny." The bunny wasted much time trying to run away from the pursuing love of his mother.

Running from God is a learned behavior. As we get older our understanding of God is altered from a God who is present with us, pursuing us, to a God who is distant—a God who only shows up on Sunday mornings at church. Instead of a God who is running after us, trying to get our attention, we begin to run after God, trying to get God's attention.

Psalm 139 is pretty clear. We don't need to run after God's attention—we already have it. In verse 7 David laments:

Where can I go from your Spirit?
Where can I flee from your presence?

God is present with us. But God is more than present with us, He *knows* us. He doesn't follow alongside of us, He follows *inside* of us. We don't have to attend church to find God. We don't have to make sure our life is clear of any sin to find God.

God has found us regardless of our situation, regardless of our condition. We can be lost, dizzied by our own spiritual vertigo, but God is present with us, luring us back to Himself. We may turn our backs on God, but God is always facing us.

SAVORING

Truth is so obvious, we not only stop seeing it but we ignore it as well. If we want to hear God we have to listen, and yet the one deficiency epidemic among adults is listening. We don't listen. We won't listen. We are willing to do almost anything to keep ourselves from listening. Tell me to acquire a new skill. Tell me to get involved in a new activity. Suggest a new book or tape or place to see. But please don't tell me to listen.

I would like to suggest a new way of hearing God's whisper—savoring. Savoring is the lost art of cherishing, appreciating, relishing. When you and I stop and savor a particular of life, we soak it in, we listen with all of our senses, we immerse ourselves in what we are savoring.

When my first grandchild, Noah, was born, I was lucky enough to get to the hospital before he was twenty-four hours old. Mom and Dad were pretty worn out from the birthing experience, so I volunteered to take the baby while they took a break. Alone with my grandson, I sat in the rocker and rocked him to sleep for a very long time. While he was sleeping in my arms, I couldn't take my eyes off him. I was fascinated by his tinyness, by the perfect shaping of his fingers and arms, his nose and ears. He had a distinct smell, the fragrance of new life, the lingering after-fragrance of the womb fluids. My senses were electrified. I noticed everything. Nothing about Noah escaped my awareness. The experience was intoxicating. Oh, the joys of grandparenting! That day I realized savoring was a very important part of life that I had been missing. Savoring takes time. Savoring requires our full attention. Savoring utilizes all of us.

If we truly want to hear God, if we truly want to hear Him

speak, then we need to take the time to savor Him. To immerse ourselves in our Father and bask in the intoxicating presence of God's speaking voice—this is prayer. Prayer is savoring God. Savoring is *immersing* ourselves in His presence, hearing Him with all of our senses.

WAITING

One attribute of children that does not leave us when we get older is the inability to wait. Not waiting is a childlike quality that haunts us all of our lives. In the American culture we are encouraged not to wait. We are told that most of life's problems can be fixed, and fixed quickly. We are more than a fast-food society, we are a fast-fix society, and if we have a problem hearing God, there are plenty of places promising immediate solutions, instant cures. The benefits of the gospel have been adapted to fit our quick-fix culture so that we fully expect God to change our lives instantly. In many Christian environments, we are told that God wants to give us what we need and want immediately. If you have to wait for God's blessing, these people say, you are doing something wrong because God would never want you to wait for anything. Add to this quick-fix gospel the notion that waiting is a waste of time, and you have the foundation laid for churches full of impatient, demanding Christians who want and expect God to meet their every "need" now.

Trouble is, God doesn't work that way. "God is faithful, but He's slow," says my friend Devlin Donaldson. We don't want a slow God, we don't want to wait. Sue Monk Kidd, a writer who is an admitted quickaholic, describes how a monk responded to her resistance to waiting:

When you are waiting you are not doing nothing.
You're doing something. You're allowing your soul to
grow up. If you can't be still and wait, you can't
become what God created you to be.[6]

We will hear the whispering God *if* we are willing to wait, if we are willing to abandon our need for the quick fix. "God is our midwife not our rescuer,"[7] Sue reminds us.

In C. S. Lewis's *The Horse and His Boy* Shasta is lost, frightened, and most of all, exhausted. His predicament has him depressed and feeling sorry for himself. Seated on his horse, Bree, he is wandering in the pitch dark up a winding, narrow, mountain trail. In the midst of his funk he is startled by a new awareness.

> Shasta discovered that someone or somebody was walking beside him. It was pitch dark and he could see nothing. And the Thing (or Person) was going so quietly that he could hardly hear any footfalls. What he could hear was breathing. His invisible companion seemed to breathe on a very large scale, and Shasta got the impression that it was a very large creature. And he had come to notice his breathing so gradually that he had really no idea how long it had been there. It was a horrible shock.

Eventually Shasta hears the warm breath speak and begins a very intense conversation with this breath. At the end of the conversation Shasta is no longer afraid . . . sort of.

> Shasta was no longer afraid that the Voice belonged to something that would eat him, nor that it was the voice of a ghost. But a new and different sort of trembling came over him. Yet he felt glad too.[8]

Elijah was depressed and lonely, too, but God was not in his successes with the prophets of Baal. God was not in the dazzling firestorms and earthquakes. God was in the thin silence that whispers to all of us, "My child, I've been waiting for you with outstretched arms."

CHAPTER SIX

Irresponsible Passion

*I'm discovering that a spiritual journey is a lot like a poem.
You don't merely recite a poem or analyze it intellectually.
You dance it, sing it, cry it, feel it on your skin and in your
bones. You move with it and feel its caress. It falls on you
like a teardrop or wraps around you like a smile. It lives in
the heart and the body as well as the spirit and the head.[1]*

*You called, you cried, you shattered my deafness.
You sparkled, you blazed, you drove away my blindness.
You shed your fragrance, and I drew in my breath, and I
pant for you. I tasted and I now hunger and thirst.
You touched me, and I now burn with longing
for your peace.[2]*

*Just when I get my church all sorted out,
sheep from the goats, saved from the damned,
hopeless from the hopeful, somebody makes a move,
gets out of focus, cuts loose, and I see why Jesus never wrote
systematic theology. So you and I can give thanks that the
locus of Christian thinking appears to be shifting from
North America and northern Europe where people write
rules and obey them, to places like Africa and Latin
American where people still know how to dance.[3]*

*"Again, the kingdom of heaven is like a merchant looking
for fine pearls. When he found one of great value, he went
away and sold everything he had and bought it."[4]*

W HAT DOES IT MEAN TO LIVE A PASSIONATE LIFE?
For as long as I can remember, I was told the Christian life was like a mountaintop. We lived most of our lives down in the valley, except for those times of retreat or special conferences where we actually experienced the presence of God. Everyone would conclude the conference with the admonition, "You've been on the mountaintop this weekend, and now you're going back down to the valley." The goal was to learn to experience God in the valley just as we did on the mountaintop, but it never seemed to work. So I grew up believing the Christian life was a series of ups and downs, valleys and mountaintops, and that as I grew older I would have fewer ups and downs and the whole cycle of valleys and mountaintops would move closer to God. Eventually, if I lived long enough, I would reach the mountaintop permanently.

The mountaintop/valley view of life is seriously flawed—it's one-dimensional and inadequate. Now I believe roller coasters are a more accurate model of the Christian life. You say yes to Jesus, and suddenly you are strapped in and you think, *I'm going to die!* Then you begin the long climb of growth—Sunday school, baptism, church membership—and you think, *Hey, no problem. I can follow Jesus anywhere*, and then—ZOOOOOOOOM—you crash into the twists and turns of life, jerking left then right, up then down, and fifty, sixty years go by and—*WHAM!*—you're dead. I have used the roller coaster as my model for many years now, and I often say to people, "If I were to have a heart attack right at this moment, I hope I would have just enough air in my lungs and just enough strength in me to utter one last sentence as I fell to the floor: *"What a ride!"* My life has been up and down, careening left then right, full of mistakes and bad decisions, and if I died right now, even though I would love to live longer, I could say from the depths of my soul, "What a ride!"

Passion is the roller coaster ride that can happen when you follow Jesus Christ. It is the breathtaking, thrill-filled, bone-rattling ride of a lifetime where every moment matters and all you can do is hang on for life dear. When you become a Christian, when you decide to follow Christ, you decide in favor of passion. Jesus came to forgive us of our sin, yes, but His mission was also to introduce us to the passion of living. Most people believe that following Jesus is all about living *right. Not true.* Following Jesus is all about living *fully.* Listen carefully to the apostle Paul's description of the Christian life to the church in Rome.

> It stands to reason, doesn't it, that if the alive-and-present God who raised Jesus from the dead moves into your life, he'll do the same thing in you that he did in Jesus, bringing you alive to himself? When God lives and breathes in you (and he does, as surely as he did in Jesus), *you are delivered from that dead life.* With his Spirit living in you, your body will be as alive as Christ's! . . .
>
> This resurrection life you received from God is not a timid, grave-tending life. It's adventurously expectant, greeting God with a childlike "What's next, Papa?" (Romans 8:10-11,15, MSG, emphasis added)

What is passion? Aliveness. Living with expectancy, anticipation, and enthusiasm.

What is the opposite of passion? Dead living. Living a life that is borrrrring!

JUST ANOTHER TELEPHONE POLE

A friend of mine was telling me about his minister, who for thirty-five years pastored the same church. He was retiring in six months, and my friend asked him how it felt to be stepping down. Would he miss the pulpit? The preaching? The minister startled my friend with this reply:

I retire from this church in six months — twenty-three Sundays, to be exact. Have you ever driven across Arizona or Nevada in the middle of the desert? Your car is speeding along on a road that seems to stretch forever in front of you, and, depending on how fast you are going, a telephone pole swishes by you every few seconds. Every Sunday, after my sermon is over I think to myself, *another telephone pole.*

My friend and I looked at each other in shock. *Another telephone pole?* Thirty-five years in the ministry and all you can say about each Sunday is that you are one telephone pole closer to retirement? The man should have resigned a long time ago. He was bored. His passion was gone.

One Sunday morning after church I was talking with an elderly woman who was visiting. During the get-acquainted dialogue I asked about her husband. "Oh," she said, "he passed away a year ago."

"I'm sorry," I said meekly. "How long had you two been married?"

"Forty years," she said in a dull monotone.

"*Forty years?* You must miss him terribly."

"I wish I did," she whispered, "but I have come to terms with the fact that in forty years of marriage I never knew him."

Imagine. Forty years of being together, sleeping together, having children together, celebrating grandchildren together, and all you can say at the end is, "I never knew him." Forty years of a passionless marriage where two people are strangers to one another.

The absence of passion results in a grim pallor over our lives, the absence of highs and lows. When there is no passion, we live our lives in the smoky fog of sameness. Life loses its distinctions and we no longer see the nuances, the tiny differences. We no longer feel our feelings. They become dull and insensitive. Life without passion is life without texture, contrast, and depth. We walk through life trancelike, going through the motions of living, emotionless, getting through each day, getting *by*, ending our lives lost and directionless, busy doing something that turns out to be nothing, focusing on what doesn't matter, missing what does.

Where Has All the Passion Gone?

I believe most of us have lost our passion: the passion of our marriages, the passion of our jobs, and the passion of our faith. A friend of mine invited me to speak at a Northern California Toastmasters Convention. When I was young I was very active in Toastmasters (a secular business club to teach men and women how to speak publicly), so I was very happy to accept. Six months later, I had forgotten all about the event when my friend called to remind me. The event was a two-hour drive away, and he called me about two hours before I was to be there. I jumped in my car and drove intensely, but I was relaxed because of my many years of speaking experience. I would just talk about what I've learned about speaking over the years. I arrived ten minutes before I was to speak. My friend Tom breathed a sigh of relief and then began to prepare me. "Remember, Mike," he said, "you are giving the keynote address."

"No problem," I said. "But remind me again what areas these people are from."

"Well," Tom said hurriedly, "they are the postmasters from every city in northern California."

I interrupted. "What did you say?"

He said, "These are the postmasters fro—"

"*Postmasters!* I thought you said *Toast*masters!"

"No," Tom said. "Why would I say that? I *am* a postmaster, you know."

In two minutes I would be speaking to a roomful of postmasters. On my way up to the podium I decided in desperation to talk about something I frequently talk about: the loss of passion. It was one of the most rewarding experiences I have ever had. Halfway through my talk, people were crying throughout the audience. When I was done, they all rose to their feet to underscore my call to rediscover passion. They were expecting a lecture on stamp regulations and I was expecting to talk about using voice inflection and gestures, but just under the surface, a group of postmasters got in touch with their longings for passion again.

RECOVERING OUR PASSION

How do we recover our passion?

I believe there are three roads that lead us back to passion: recognizing, receiving, and risking.

Recognizing the Passion of Jesus

One of many famous stories in the Bible is that of the prodigal son, and there is a reason why it is famous: because every time we hear this story, we *remember!* Somewhere deep inside us there is a stirring, a longing, a remembering, a sense of loss, a wanting we didn't know was present.

There are two sons in this story, and the younger son demands his inheritance now: a huge insult to his father; a rash and destructive choice for himself. The father gives in. (Interesting, isn't it? The father allows his son to make a bad decision. He knows exactly what his son is going to do with the money, but he allows him to take the money anyway. Good fathers know they have to let their children go. But that is another book.) The son parties and wastes the money and soon is penniless, homeless, and living in a pigpen. He finally decides to make the humiliating return home and ask his father for a servant's job. This is where we all begin to love this story.

The father has never recovered from the loss of his son. Hurt deeply, he obviously spends much of his day staring out into the barren, desolate landscape, mourning the loss of his son. It is a grief that makes each day colorless, a grief that quickens his eyesight and his hearing. Every day he looks for his son, and every night he listens for his son.

One day he sees a tiny speck on the horizon. He knows that speck, even at a great distance—he *knows* the walk, the gait, the slumped shoulders, the head hung in despair. The son is not even looking for his father—he doesn't expect him. But his father is looking for him, loving him closer until he cannot stand the wait. He rushes out, his short stocky body strong, toughened by many years and by much grief, until at a dead run he embraces his son, locking his thick dark arms around the weakened shadow of what was once a wild and passionate boy. Not realizing how fast he is running, the father knocks his boy over and together they roll, laughing, crying, holding each other tighter than either of them has ever been held. "Kill the calf! Get the robe and the ring. We are having a party tonight! My son is back. My son is back."

I love this story. I love the *passion* of the father for his son ... but ... but ... the voices start in me just as they did with the older brother. "You can't just forgive him! He should suffer consequences for his behavior. You can't let him get away with this. He'll just do it again! It's not fair, especially to the older brother!" But the father ignores all the voices, acts totally irresponsibly, and throws a party.

All of my religious life I have been told how much God loves me, but the good news was always accompanied by bad news. Yes, God loves you, but His love has conditions:

You must love back.
You must live a life worthy of His love.
You must respond to His love with responsible, normal behavior.

The message was mixed. God loves me unconditionally.... Yet as His child I had to live up to what others claimed were God's standards.

98

I had no idea that God's love was extravagant, irresponsible . . . and irresistible. I had no idea the God of the universe
loved me with no conditions, no addenda to the contract, no
fine print. I had no idea God was passionate about *me!* His passion for *me*, His love for *me*, makes me want to love like *Him*.
Passion is much harder than legalism. The behavior of the
father appears to be irresponsible, but his passion is irresistible,
staggering, compelling—the young man is loved to his senses.
It was an act of pure passion.

A young father, a typical type-A personality, followed the
same routine every workday. He would arrive home around
5:30 P.M., park the car in the garage, walk out to the driveway
with briefcase in hand, pick up the newspaper, proceed to the
front door, enter the house, place the briefcase in the hallway,
put the newspaper on the couch in the living room, then walk
down the long hallway to the kitchen. Once in the kitchen, he
would open the cupboard, take out a glass, and place it on the
counter. He would then open the refrigerator, reach for the car-
ton of milk, walk over to the glass, pour the glass full of milk,
and return the milk to the refrigerator. Without thinking, he
would pick up the glass of cold milk, grab a cookie from the
cookie jar on the counter, and walk to the living room where
he would sit down, power up the television with the remote,
and watch the news while drinking his milk and eating his
cookie, sometimes stopping during commercials to browse
through the newspaper. His routine had been the same for
many years, and, unbeknownst to him, his three-year-old son
had noticed.

One night the father came home from work and began his
usual routine. As he stepped into the hallway, setting his briefcase and newspaper down, he looked up to see his son standing down the hall, a smile on his face, obviously anticipating
his father's return. Dad knew something was up, so he stopped
and watched his son turn around and head for the kitchen.
Pleasantly surprised, the dad crept to the edge of the kitchen
to see what his son was up to. The little boy ran to the corner

of the kitchen, pulled out the bottom drawer (which he was not supposed to do), stepped on the drawer, climbed onto the counter (which he was not supposed to do), reached into the cupboard, and pulled on a glass, knocking the other glasses over. Thankfully, none of them broke. With glass in hand, the little boy scooted back down onto the drawer, then to the floor, and ran over to the cookie jar. He reached up as high as he could and, barely grasping the jar, knocked it over and spilled cookies all over the floor. Oblivious to his father, he scooped all the cookies up and put them back on the counter, except for one. He picked up the remaining cookie, ran over to the refrigerator, placed the cookie and the empty glass on the floor, opened the refrigerator door, and reached inside and grabbed the plastic half-gallon container of milk. Awfully heavy for a three-year-old, it promptly fell to the floor, which knocked the top off and spilled a little milk. He then picked up the container of milk and, the container wobbling terribly, began to pour the milk into the glass, spilling milk all over the floor. Any other evening the father would have yelled at his son by this time, pointing out the terrible mess he was making. Instead, he sensed something much more important was happening here; he patiently waited as the little boy picked up the cookie and the glass of milk and came running to him with a huge smile on his face. The dad threw his arms around his son and said, "Thank you, Son!" Dad realized his son was giving him a wonderful gift.[5]

This three-year-old boy had acted purely out of passion for his father and, luckily, his father had recognized it. Normally by the time little boys are three, the passion has been learned out of them, and by the time they're big boys, it's a forgotten luxury of childhood.

As you read this story, I am sure the voices of neatness and order and responsibility were screaming, "Don't step on the drawer! Get off the counter! Look out, you're going to break those glasses! Look at the mess you've made on the floor! You're spilling milk everywhere!" If the father had listened to those voices, who knows what damage would have been done to his son. The passionate love of the son revealed the passionate love of the Father, whose only response was gratitude.

How many years of my life I have pictured God standing at the door of the kitchen, saying, "Mike, put the glass down! Stop doing that! Get off the counter!" I had no idea that as I stumbled up to God with my milk and cookies, the kitchen of my life in disarray, God was loving me, spilled milk and all, *and* opening His arms, saying, "Thank you, Michael. You are such a gift to Me!" Not only does the passionate love of God fill us with passion, it fills us with gratitude.

Receiving the Gift of Gratitude

One of the most moving stories in the New Testament is recorded in all four Gospels. Jesus was having a meal at the home of Simon the Leper. Many people were there, including some of the disciples, when a woman barged in uninvited and poured expensive perfume on Jesus. Shock and anger swept through the room like a tidal wave. "How dare you waste such expensive perfume," the guests chided. "You could have sold the perfume for more than a year's wages and given the money to the poor!"

Jesus cared very much for the poor, but He knew passion when He saw it, and He placed a very high value on it indeed. "Leave her alone!" He shot back. "Do you see this woman? I came into your house. You did not give Me any water for My feet, but she wet My feet with her tears and wiped them with her hair. You did not give Me a kiss, but this woman, from the time I entered, has not stopped kissing My feet. You did not put oil on My head, but she has poured perfume on My feet!"

Jesus predicted that this woman would be remembered for her passion. And she is. Everyone else in that room could have cared less about passion. They were interested in the bottom line. The woman was not only grateful, she was *overflowing* with gratitude, so much so that her eyes could not contain her passion.

Passion is extravagant.

Passion can't be fabricated or manipulated. Passion springs from gratitude.

A close friend of ours is in the music business. For ten years he and his wife lived out of a suitcase or, as he became more successful, out of a bus. Finally, the wife suggested firmly that it might be nice to settle down and have a real home, complete with yard, running water, and a bathtub. She had dreamed of a home for years, and within a few months fell in love with an old fixer-upper that she and her husband were able to renovate and customize to their own needs. It was small, but perfect for them.

They were so happy and wanted to share their happiness with as many of their friends as possible, so they organized a home dedication. Each person or couple who came brought a portion of dirt from their own yard along with a verbal blessing for our friends. As they gave their blessing, they poured their dirt into a large pail to mingle with everyone else's. The community dirt was then mixed with the dirt of our friends' garden. I was honored to be asked to give the final blessing of the evening. Here are the words I read:

> In less than a week, Steve and Debbie will live here. And it will be like a dream, won't it? We can all see them as they lie together in their bed after we have all gone, illuminated in the shadows by the glow of the moon, holding each other in the silent embrace of their longtime dream. And then, Steve and Debbie slowly, gently, your eyes will fill with tears, and you will both whisper to each other, "I can't believe it. I can't believe it!"

Such is the cry of gratitude. And when we have truly been embraced by the passionate love of Jesus, we wake up each morning and our eyes mist up and we look to God and say gently, "I can't believe it. I can't believe it!"

Take the Risk to Live Passionately

Passion is always risky. The Bible gives example after example of people who fell in love with Jesus and left their jobs, their families, their security. Once people met Jesus, their passion became hazardous to their health. People were estranged from the church and rejected by their parents; they became unemployed suddenly, ended up in jail, lost their lives, became *personae non gratae*, and were accused of being drunkards. Passion is not something to be treated lightly. The passionate life is a risky life. The question is, Is the passionate life worth the risk?

A young girl graduated from high school somewhat unsure of her future. After taking a year off, she enrolled in the university to begin her college career. Her parents breathed a sigh of relief. But after a year and a half at college, she wasn't happy or settled. She decided to drop out of school and live in Hawaii for a year. Her parents and grandparents were concerned. "Careful," they counseled. "A college education is essential in the modern world. Hawaii is great, but how will you earn a living after college?"

She went to Hawaii and loved every minute of her experience, and when she returned to the mainland she postponed her education even longer to live in Lake Tahoe, where the snowboarding was good. Her parents and grandparents were even more concerned. "Uh . . . Hawaii and Tahoe are wonderful resorts and fun places to live, but don't forget your education. You are twenty-two and you are not getting any younger."

What the parents and grandparents didn't understand was that while this young girl was "wasting her time in resorts," she was traipsing around in her soul, searching for God. Although her father was a minister, she had never fully embraced Christianity. It wasn't that she didn't *believe* in God, it was more a matter of knowing. She didn't *know* God, and she certainly didn't understand the love of God. Of course, her parents knew nothing of her inner journey. She kept telling them she was going to return to school the next year. Then they received the phone call. "I'm not going back to school next year. I'm going to Africa!"

"*Africa?* Why on earth would you be going to Africa?" Her parents were more than a little concerned.

"I want to find God. I am going to spend five months on the Mercy Ship which is now in South Africa."

The parents were shocked and asked the typical questions: "How much will it cost? How will you find the money?"

"No problem," she said confidently. "I have been saving money and I will write a few people to see if they will help me."

In two months she had raised the money and was in South Africa on the Mercy Ship. It was a five-month adventure. She and a group of others were the first white people to live in a black shantytown just outside of Durban. In her newsletter explaining her trip to the people who supported her, she wrote,

> It was around midnight, and my friend Carolyn and I were sitting on top of a jungle gym (in Canaan) talking about how quickly our time in South Africa had gone. The moon was shining through a thin slice of clouds, and the stars were shining almost as brightly as they do in my hometown. The wind was blowing some Eucalyptus trees, and Carolyn and I were bundled up in sweatshirts and dirt covered skirts. "I've fallen in love," I told Carolyn. "I've fallen in love, and I am never falling out." I will never forget that night, the trees, the wind, the smells. I had broken out of my eggshell, emerged from my cocoon, and I was ready to tell the world that I had fallen in love. I had found what I was looking for, and when I found Him He hadn't moved. He wasn't lost. He just embraced me and said, "Thank you, thank you. I have loved you all along, Jill. All this time, I loved you first." What an amazing love!

The girl who wrote the letter was our daughter, Jill! She wasn't going to college. She wasn't pursuing a career. She was risking her future on her search for God. And *she found Him!*

Go ahead, live irresponsibly! Forget about what is sensible, responsible, and prudent and rediscover the childlike passion of falling in love with God. Take the ride of your life on the roller coaster of His unconditional love. Go ahead, say it: *What a ride!*

CHAPTER SEVEN

Happy Terror

*Those who are really serious about their religion and want
to become the kind of person that God wants them to be are
the ones most in danger.*[1]

*A tremor seizes our limbs; our nerves are struck, quiver
like strings; our whole being bursts into shudders. But then
a cry, wrested from our very core, fills the world around
us, as if a mountain were suddenly about to place itself in
front of us. It is one word: GOD. Not an emotion, a stir
within us, but a power, a marvel beyond us, tearing the
world apart.*[2]

WHEN MY TWO BOYS WERE VERY YOUNG, WE USED TO PLAY hide-and-seek in the house. I would count to ten and search for my sons. After I found them, we would reverse roles: Mark, the four-year-old, would lead Trent, the two-year-old, on a search for Dad. I added another dimension to the game besides hiding and seeking, however—total fear. A few seconds before my boys discovered me, I would leap out from my hiding place, screaming, and scare the socks off them. It made the game much more interesting. Finding Dad was one dimension, surviving the scare was the bigger challenge.

One night, after I had successfully found their hiding places, I hid behind the door of the bedroom. When they finished counting to a thousand (fear is an effective deterrent of short counts), they started searching the kitchen. "He's in the walk-in pantry," the older boy announced.

"Then you look," said the younger son.

"No, *you* look," responded the older.

"Okay, we'll both look!" And both of them held hands and slowly opened the pantry door. Of course, I wasn't there, so I did what all fathers (and mothers) do when their children are not finding them. I yelled. Startled, the older boy whispered, "He's not in the pantry."

Both the boys immediately set off in the direction of the yell and saw the bedroom door partially opened. The room was dark; the light switch was within reach, but they ignored it. Slowly they crept into the room. When I saw the top of my older boy's head, I leaped out from behind the door and screamed. Both boys jumped about two feet in the air, screamed, and began tripping over each other trying to get away from the screaming monster. Suddenly my older boy stopped, put his arms around his little brother, calmed them both down, looked up at their father waving his hands and growling like the Abominable Snowman, and said with a twinkle in his eye, "HEY! He isn't a monster. It's our dad! Attack!" And they did.

Two small boys, terrified of their father . . . except they weren't. When they walked into the room their hearts were pounding; they knew this "thing" was about to pounce on them. They knew the strength of this "monster," but they also knew the love of this monster. They knew the approximate whereabouts of their father because they had heard a noise coming from one part of the house, but they didn't know exactly where he was. Nevertheless, they were drawn to him like a magnet. They sought him out, refusing to turn on the light, and when he finally did pounce on them, they started to run until it dawned on them: *Wait a minute. This scary presence is our dad.* In a small way my two boys experienced terror, the same kind of childlike terror we should all experience in the presence of our Father.

WHAT HAPPENED TO TERROR?

I don't see much terror today among followers of Christ. In fact, when I say that, people look at me as if I'm crazy. Well, I want to know what happened to the bone-chilling, earth-shattering, gut-wrenching, knee-knocking, heart-stopping, life-altering fear that leaves us speechless, paralyzed, helpless, and glad. The terror I am speaking of is a mix of wonder, awe, fear, and worship, all happening at the same time.

I am beginning to wonder if we modern followers of Christ are capable of being terrified of God. No fear of God. No fear of Jesus. No fear of the Holy Spirit. As a result, we have ended up with a feel-good gospel that attracts thousands . . . but transforms no one.

It is time for Christianity to become a place of terror again; a place where God continually has to tell us, "Fear not"; a place where our relationship with God is not a simple belief or doctrine or theology, but the constant awareness of God's terrifying presence in our lives. The nice, nonthreatening God needs to be replaced by the God whose very presence smashes our egos into dust, burns our sin into ashes, and strips us naked to reveal the real person within. A healthy, childlike fear should make us more in awe of God than we are of our government, our problems, our beliefs about abortion, our doctrines and agendas, or any of our other earthly concerns. Our God is perfectly capable of both calming the storm and putting us in the middle of one. Either way, if it's God, we will be speechless and trembling . . . and smiling, too. It's time to become people whose God is big and holy and frightening and gentle and tender and *ours*; a God whose love frightens us into His strong and powerful arms where He dares to hold us in His terrifying, loving presence.

How did we end up so comfortable with God? How did our awe of God get reduced to a lukewarm appreciation of God? How did God become a pal instead of a heart-stopping presence? How can we think of Jesus without remembering His ground-shaking, thunder-crashing, stormy exit on the cross? Why aren't we continually catching our breath and saying, "This is no ordinary God!"?

COMFORT WITH THE FAMILIAR

Most American Christians are too familiar with Christianity. After all, this is a "Christian nation." A large percentage of Americans still attend church on a fairly regular basis. We know about God and Jesus and the Bible. We've heard the stories, sung the songs, gone to Sunday school, been baptized and confirmed. We know all about God. God is part of our culture, part of our upbringing, part of our daily lives.

I recently realized just how dangerous it can be to become comfortable with what's familiar. I travel to Belfast, Northern Ireland, every other year and have fallen in love with this broken nation. I love the people of Northern Ireland, and every time I am there my heart is broken over the "troubles" that continue to tear apart this tiny country. On my first visit I was met at the airport by a bright, engaging, college-age young man. After we loaded my luggage in the car and headed for my hotel, I asked him, "How do you manage to live in the midst of daily bombings and shootings? Do you ever get used to it?"

He smiled and said, "You Americans. You watch too much television. There is more crime in one day in New York than there is in an entire year in Belfast."

"Oh," I said. I had no idea. About thirty minutes away from my hotel I asked the young man what my hotel was like.

He smiled again. "Oh, I'm sorry. I guess we forgot to tell you, the original hotel you were booked in was blown up about a month ago. We had to change your hotel."

Okay, I thought. *Fine. I can handle this.* When we arrived in Portadown at my new hotel, I asked the college student if he knew of a small market downtown where I could buy some snacks for my three-day stay.

"I'm afraid there is no market. A bomb exploded downtown about three days ago, and it will be months before all the damage is repaired. Besides, there is a curfew at 6 P.M., so you won't be able to leave the hotel anyway."

"Okay, I can deal with this," I kept saying to myself.

The next morning the young man drove me to the festival where I would be speaking. On the way there, on a narrow, winding country road, two camouflaged soldiers with two very large machine guns suddenly stepped into the middle of the road and motioned for us to stop. Our IDs were checked with one machine gun pointed at my head and another pointed at the driver's head. The driver was fine; I was totally shaken. I thought, *Uh, yeah, this is just like New York.*

What dawned on me later was that the people of the sad country of Northern Ireland have lived with terror so long *they no longer recognize it.* They have become oblivious to a terror that can *destroy* them.

Ironically, our "Christian" nation has become oblivious to a terror that can *liberate* us. We have become *comfortable* with the radical truth of the gospel; we have become familiar with Jesus; we have become satisfied with the church. The quick and sharp Bible has become slow and dull; the world-changing church has become changed by the world; and the life-threatening Jesus has become an interesting enhancement to modern life.

If Jesus *is* the Son of God, we should be terrified of what He will do when He gets His hands on our lives; if the Bible *is* the Word of God, we should be quaking every time we read its soul-piercing words; if the church *is* the body of Christ, our culture should be threatened by our intimidating presence. But our culture is *not* threatened by our presence; it's not terrified of the Jesus in our lives; and it's not quaking at the Word of God. Why? Because we have familiarized the gospel, sanitized it, flattened it, taken the sting and the terror out of it. We've been intimidated by those who claim to be familiar with Jesus. Whether they be preachers, teachers, or writers, these familiarizers convince us that their familiarity with God gives them a special knowledge of how and when God works. At first glance these people seem to know God extremely well. They seem to know all about God. They know the "Key to God's Will" or "How to Live a Happy Life" or "Six Steps to Maturity." Although they would never claim special status with God, one gets the impression (an impression which is not discouraged) that these ministers, teachers, and writers do have a special status with God. Their message is, "Become more *familiar* with God and the Bible; then you will know what God is up to just like we do." That message couldn't be further from the truth.

These people have reduced the gospel to a set of principles, Bible verses, moral absolutes, and theorems—as though God were some kind of mathematical problem that needed to be solved. What is implied (but never said) is that once we understand the formula, once we have determined "God's principles," then we can be comfortable because we know how God works. Which makes great sense . . . unless they are wrong.

The disciples were very familiar with Jesus. They knew Him inside and out. Or so they thought. Jesus had spent a long day in ministry, Mark tells us (Mark 6:45-52), and He decided to send the disciples on ahead while He went up a mountainside to pray. While they were rowing their boat to the other side of the Sea of Galilee, the winds picked up and the water became rough. The disciples were making little headway. Sometime after three in the morning, they looked up and saw Jesus walking on the water. At first they thought He was a ghost, but then "They cried out, because they all saw him and were *terrified*" (verse 50, emphasis added).

The disciples had been with Jesus for two years. They had seen miracles, healings, and people brought back from the dead, and still they were terrified when they saw Him on the water. If anyone should have been able to identify Jesus, the disciples should have. If anyone should have understood the power Jesus possessed, they should have. *But they thought Jesus was a ghost.* It was an incident of mistaken identity. They thought they knew all there was to know about Jesus, but the Jesus they knew was small and the Jesus on the water was much bigger than they ever imagined.

When you and I are in the presence of the mysterious Son of God, the mystery becomes more mysterious. God does not shrink when we know Him, He expands. God does not become smaller, He becomes bigger. The apostle Paul makes it perfectly clear in 1 Corinthians 13: "We see but a poor reflection as in a mirror." In other words, the "poor reflection" is the description of our understanding and knowledge of God now. "Now we know in part," Paul says. But "then" we will see clearly. "Then" we shall know fully. The "then" Paul is talking about isn't now. When we are with God, "then" the veil will be lifted. Too many of us want the "then" to be now. The mysterious, marvelous fear we feel in the presence of God is a sign of maturity; it's a sign of intimacy, of a deep and abiding faith. It is the moment when we understand the "ghost" (the monster) is really our daddy.

Darkness Makes God Scarier *and* Closer

Darkness is a breeding ground of fear. When we are in the dark, we can't see anyone or anything. We feel panicky, helpless, isolated, vulnerable, lost, confused, frightened. Most of all, what we feel is alone. Darkness isolates us; it disorients us and causes us to exaggerate and distort reality. The disciples were desperate in their boat. They were overcome with panic and confusion. The darkness made Jesus hard to see.

In C. S. Lewis's *The Voyage of the Dawn Treader*, the *Dawn Treader* has sailed into Dark Island and everyone on the boat is terrified (much like the disciples in their boat were), except for a lone courageous mouse named Reepicheep. At one point in their journey, when it looks as though they'll never get out of Dark Island, Lucy, one of the visitors to Narnia, whispers, "Aslan, Aslan, if ever you loved us at all, send us help now." Lewis writes, "The darkness did not grow any less, but she began to feel a little—a very, very little—better." Almost immediately one of the crew spots a tiny speck of light ahead, which, again, "did not alter the surrounding darkness" but did light up the ship. (Notice that the darkness did not diminish. God does not always rid us of the darkness; He joins us in the darkness.)

> Lucy looked along the beam [speck of light] and presently saw something in it. At first it looked like a cross, then it looked like an aeroplane, then it looked like a kite, and at last with a whirring of wings it was right overhead and was an albatross. It circled three times round the mast and then perched for an instant on the crest of the gilded dragon at the prow. It called

out in a strong sweet voice what seemed to be words
though no one understood them. . . . But no one except
Lucy knew that as it circled the mast it had whispered
to her, "Courage, dear heart," and the voice, she felt
sure, was Aslan's and with the voice a delicious smell
breathed in her face.[3]

When the disciples saw Jesus, they were terrified. But in the
midst of their terror they heard Jesus whisper, "Take courage!
It is I. Don't be afraid" (sounds very similar to "Courage, dear
heart," doesn't it?), and then He climbed into the boat with
them. What did the disciples do then? Matthew tells us they
worshiped Him. The winds were still blowing, the disciples
were still struggling with rowing, but Jesus was in the boat—
and they worshiped Him. Their worship was a direct result of
their experience with Jesus *in the dark*. Now the disciples knew
Jesus even better. They understood now, but only now, that
when life gets dark, when we are alone, *we aren't alone*. Jesus
Christ is Lord even in the darkness.

TERROR OF THE COMPLICATED

A friend of mine picked up his second-grade daughter from her
Christian school. As they were driving home my friend asked,
"What did you learn in school today?"

"I learned about the bees, Daddy."

"Oh?" the father replied. "What did you learn?"

"My teacher said that God made the bee and the Devil
made the stinger."

My friend, and rightly so, was very concerned with the
teacher's understanding of reality. Attributing all good things
to God and all bad things to the Devil appears to make life
much easier to understand. No complications here. No mystery to unravel, no difficult issues to resolve. God is easy to
understand and easy to decipher. There's nothing to be afraid
of when you're around a God who is easy to understand.

But the teacher was wrong. God made the bee, *and He made the stinger!* We are living in a world where bee stings can kill us, and that is scary. Reality is complicated, life is complicated, God is complicated. His footprints are not easy to see in the dust and dirt of the real world's trail. And when we are lost in the forest, we want to find God's tracks. When it's dark and we're stuck in a boat during a gale, we don't want dark, indistinguishable shapes roaming around on the water. We get frightened when we lose track of God. We get terrified when we are not sure what God is doing.

But here is the good news. Remember my two sons? Remember when they came to the bedroom and knew I was hiding in the darkness? They could have turned on the light, *but they didn't!* As terrified as they were of the "monster" lurking in the dark, they could not stop themselves because intuitively they knew Daddy was in there, too. One of the glorious complications of God is His ability to reveal Himself in the unrevealable. God is not lost when we are. God is waiting for us even in the darkness!

John the Baptist learned how complicated Jesus was. He had erupted across the countryside with his odd clothing, his thunderous preaching. Soon he was drawing huge crowds. "I am not the Messiah!" he would say. "But the Messiah is coming and I will introduce Him." John the Baptist was faithful to his Messiah, and he did introduce Him to the world. After that great moment he would not let his fame or the loyalty of his followers get in the way of his mission. He understood Jesus— He was the Messiah.

Then John the Baptist ended up in prison. No freedom. No crowds. No following. And no Messiah. His emotions began to spiral downward. His life begins to crumble and fall apart. *Was I just living a lie?* he thinks. *Do I really believe this stuff? Where is this Messiah? Why has He abandoned me? Why doesn't He get me out of here? He's healing the blind, the lepers, and the crippled, why isn't He getting me out of prison?* He sent his people to Jesus to get some answers.

And Jesus sent back a very strange message. "Hey, John. You are exactly right. The blind are seeing, the lame are walking, the lepers are cured, the deaf can now hear, the dead are raised, and the poor are hearing the good news." Jesus was saying, in effect, "Yes, I am the Messiah. Yes, I am healing the sick and raising the dead. And, no, I am not getting you out of prison. Life is complicated, John."

Surely John the Baptist must have thought Jesus would find a way to get him out of prison. No problem for Jesus to shake the prison gates free. But John was left in prison with one terrifying truth—the Jesus who can rescue you is the One you can trust even when you're not rescued. Just when John thought he knew who Jesus was, the mystery of Jesus became more mysterious. Just when John thought Jesus would prove Himself by releasing him from prison, Jesus proved Himself by leaving John in prison. Go figure.

But wait a minute. What did Jesus say to John through his messengers? He said, "John, you have staked your life on the Truth. You can trust Me, John. You can know now deep in your soul that I will be here in life, *and I will be with you in death!* Death is only the second to the last word, it is not the last word. Yes, John, your upside-down life may be coming to an end, but even death is not the end."

THE TERROR OF THE UPSIDE-DOWN LIFE

Several years ago a woman was spending her holidays on one of the barrier islands in South Carolina. It happened to be the time of year when the loggerhead turtles (huge, three-hundred-pound sea turtles) were laying their eggs. One night a very large female dragged herself onto the beach and laid her eggs. The woman did not want to disturb the turtle, so she left and came back the next morning, anxious to find where the turtle had laid her eggs. Alarmingly, what she found were some tracks heading *the wrong direction*. The turtle apparently lost her bearings and wandered into the hot sand dunes where death was certain. The woman followed the tracks and soon found the turtle covered with hot dry sand. Thinking quickly, she covered the turtle with seaweed, poured cool seawater over her, and ran to notify a park ranger. He arrived in a few minutes in a jeep. The ranger flipped the turtle over, wrapped tire chains around her front legs, and hooked the chains to the trailer hitch on the jeep. Then he drove off, dragging her through the sand so fast her mouth filled with sand and her head bent back as if it would break. At the edge of the ocean, he unhooked her and flipped her right side up. She didn't move. The water began to lap against her body, cleaning off the dry sand. When the waves were much larger, suddenly she began to move, slowly at first, and then when the water was deep enough, she pushed off into the water and disappeared.

The woman makes this observation:

> Watching her swim slowly away and remembering
> her nightmare ride through the dunes, I noticed that
> sometimes it is hard to tell whether you are being
> killed or being saved by the hands that turn your life
> upside down.[4]

All the turtle could do was hang on, and hanging on was pretty darn miserable. She could easily have died, but she lived. It must have been one terrifying ride through the dunes. If turtles can experience fear, this turtle must have done so, but it was life-giving fear, it was life-saving fear, it was the upside-down fear that always comes when we put ourselves in the hands of Jesus.

Adults don't talk about terror much. Children do all the time. They're always talking about the "boogie man" and the monster under the bed. You would think they would flee from terror any chance they have, except . . . I can still remember that every time I said to my two boys, "Want to play hide-and-seek?" they were ready to play again and again and again and. . . .

CHAPTER EIGHT

Naive Grace

Dear God,
I don't ever feel alone since I found out about you.
Nora[1]

The heart of Jesus loves us as we are and not as we should
be, beyond worthiness and unworthiness, beyond fidelity
and infidelity; He who loves us in the morning sun and the
evening rain without caution, regret, boundary, limit,
or breaking point.[2]

A few years ago I asked some friends if they would have their two-year-old daughter, Alana, color me a page out of her coloring book. When Alana colored, she never worried about lines, realism, or symmetry. It never occurred to her that something could be wrong with her work. Alana colored the page, and she brought it to me just before Sunday morning worship service. It looked like this:

She was very proud and excited, anxious for my response. I *did* respond, in the same manner I imagine most of us would respond: I *lied*. "Oh, Alana, thank you for this beautiful drawing. It must have taken you a long time and it's very special. Thank you again." Of course, part of me was thinking, *This is terrible. Is red the only color you could use? How about yellow? Blue? Green? None of your strokes are even close to being within the lines. What's the matter with you? Take this back and draw it again—only do it right this time!*

But I couldn't criticize Alana, in part because she exhibited grace, the grace of a child who knows it is okay to color outside the lines. Was she naive? Sure. Would to God we all kept our childlike naiveté about grace.

Most of my life I heard the message loud and clear that Christianity was all about coloring within the lines and coloring well. If I was a good Christian, if I loved Jesus and wanted to please Him, if I read my Bible, prayed, and went to church, then I would get better and better at coloring. And if I lived a long and godly life, I would eventually be able to draw close to the perfect drawing.

Wherever that message came from, it was a lie. I am fifty-five years old, and my coloring still looks like Alana's.

I believe God looks at my coloring and says, "Hmmmmm. You certainly like the color green! Lots of passion in this stroke. I like it."

Even as I write those words, I can hear the "concern" of those who worry about others misunderstanding the gospel. "You're not suggesting, are you, that nothing matters to God? Certainly, God has standards!"

What I am suggesting is that God's grace is so outside the lines of our understanding that we can only stand in awe and wonder. Christianity is not about learning how to live within the lines; Christianity is about the joy of coloring. The grace of God is preposterous enough to accept as beautiful a coloring that anyone else would reject as ugly. The grace of God sees beyond the scribbling to the heart of the scribbler—

a scribbler who is similar to two thieves who hung on crosses on either side of Jesus. One of the two asked Jesus to please accept his scribbled and sloppy life into the kingdom of God . . . and He did. Preposterous. And very good news for the rest of us scribblers.

GRACE LEGITIMIZES THE ILLEGITIMATE

I am not a real minister. I often refer to myself as a "Kmart minister." Never went to seminary and was asked not to return to two Bible colleges. And yet I have "pastored" a church for almost twenty years now. I am not paid by the church. Even though I joke about not being a "legitimate" minister, deep inside it has always bothered me. No one has made an issue of it intentionally, but I always sound apologetic when people find out I'm a minister and say, "Oh, you're a minister. Well, what seminary did you attend? . . . Oh, then what Bible college did you graduate from?"

A few years ago I was invited to a friend's ordination ceremony. About three hundred of us showed up on a Sunday afternoon to celebrate with him. In the Presbyterian ordination ceremony there is a "charge" to the new minister. It is a sermon strictly for that person. The audience watches and listens while the new minister is given a sermon on what it means to be a minister. Five minutes into the "charge," I was crying. I didn't know why at that moment.

At the end of the service, my friend, Ted, came forward to the front of the altar and knelt, facing the congregation. The presiding minister then invited all the ordained ministers in the audience to come forward and lay hands on Ted and pray for him. I started crying again, only now I understood why: I was not ordained. I couldn't even go forward to pray for my friend. I desperately wanted what Ted was getting. I wanted the piece of paper, the official recognition that I was a minister. I remained in my seat while fifteen or so ministers walked up to the front to pray for Ted.

While Ted was waiting for everyone to walk up front, he was savoring this moment, looking out into the crowd, sharing this moment with his friends in attendance. As he slowly scanned the room from right to left, he stopped abruptly. He was looking directly at me. He saw the tears. He smiled. I will never forget what Ted did that day. He *winked!* He looked directly into my eyes and winked, and then he gestured his head, directing me to come up front with all the other ministers. What a moment of grace! At that very moment Ted was Jesus for me. He was saying, "Mike, Jesus made you legitimate! Get up here where you belong." His wink was the wink of Jesus.

GRACE EQUALIZES THE UNEQUAL

The grace of God is dangerous. It's lavish, excessive, outrageous, and scandalous. God's grace is ridiculously inclusive. Apparently God doesn't care who He loves. He is not very careful about the people He calls His friends or the people He calls His church. Exactly.

One of my favorite parables of Jesus is found in Luke 14, the parable of the great banquet. A very wealthy man had prepared a lavish banquet and invited many guests. The day of the event, a servant is sent to tell people the feast was ready. But everyone begins to make excuses — weddings, business purchases, land deals — all legitimate reasons, and all canceling their places at the banquet.

The host is furious and makes a most preposterous decision. "Go out quickly," he says to the servant, "into the streets and alleys of the town and bring in the poor, the crippled, the blind, and the lame."

The servant obeys. Upon his return, he sheepishly says to the host, "Uh, I did what you ordered, but there's still more room."

So the master tells his servant, "Go out to the roads and country lanes and make them come in, so that my house will be full."

Can you imagine what a zoo the banquet became? Crippled, blind, lame, whores, criminals, losers, homeless, alcoholics, drug addicts, penniless, poor. A large table full of mangy, filthy, uncouth, uncivilized social rejects, none of whom was supposed to be there.

And this, we're told, is a parable of the *church!* A bunch of losers and rejects? A ragtag group of malcontents and failures? Jesus was making it very clear that there was not one iota of room in the church for arrogance because *none of us belongs in it!*

For a number of years my wife and I volunteered with a Young Life club in our town. One year a young man in our club was obviously having a difficult year. He was not doing well in school, was in and out of juvenile hall, and my wife and I struck up a friendship with him. His home was a mess. Dad was an alcoholic who emotionally and physically abused the entire family. For six months we spent a lot of time with this young man while his dad went through detox.

We would have forgotten the entire experience if it weren't for some remodeling we did on our house. We decided to redo the tile in our kitchen, and, because we live in a small town, we ordered the tile from the "big city" sixty miles away. When our special order arrived, the tile company told us they didn't have enough personnel to lay the tile for three weeks, but we could get the job done immediately if we used someone local. We had no problem with a local person, until they gave us his name.

"Absolutely not!" I yelled into the phone. "That man is an alcoholic, knocks his family around, and I don't trust him!" He was the father of the young man we had helped. Startled, the person on the phone promised to get someone else. Two days later the tile company called back with bad news. Except for this one person, everyone else was booked up. We wanted the tile done soon, so I reluctantly agreed to hire the man they recommended. I told my wife, "I am going to watch him like a hawk. He is not going to cheat me." I demanded a written

estimate, and I got one: $350 for three days' work. Each day he was laying tile, I would check on his work. On the third day it looked like he would finish on time. I walked by and said casually, "When you're done, come by my office and I'll write you a check."

"Oh," he said, "I need to talk to you about the money. I'll talk to you when I'm done."

I stormed out to my office (which is in my garage next to my wife's office) and angrily reported to my wife, "I knew it. I knew he was going to try to cheat us out of some money. Well, I have a signed contract, and I am not going to pay him one dime more than we agreed." I ranted and raved for another few minutes and then bragged to my wife, "Leave the door between our offices open so you can see how I handle this guy. I will not pay him one dime more than we agreed to."

At 5 P.M. the tile layer walked into my office, sat down directly across from my desk, and began writing out a bill. I was ready for him and glanced at my wife with the look of testosterone on my face. He started to hand me the bill, but then paused for a moment and said, "A couple of years ago I was drinking too much. I am an alcoholic and was at a very low point in my life. I almost lost my family because of my drinking. I mistreated my wife and my children, especially my oldest son. But you and your wife spent a lot of time with him at a critical moment in his life when he could have gone either way. Shortly after that time I went to AA, and I've been sober ever since. Because of you and your wife, I still have a relationship with my son. I've never been able to thank you, but I'm thanking you now." He handed me his bill for $350. "Paid in full" was written across the page. We shook hands and he walked out.

Humiliated, I slumped down in my chair, speechless. This alcoholic, abusing, untrustworthy man had just shown this arrogant, self-righteous snob the meaning of grace. I was the one who had been too busy to show up at the banquet, and he was one of the people who came. The grace of God levels us all. All of us are broken, all of us are flawed, all of us are undeserving. There's no room in the church for pride, a judgmental attitude, or arrogance. All of us have had our debt "paid in full."

GRACE GRACES EVEN OUR FAILURES

Grace is difficult to believe and difficult to accept. We want so desperately to believe that God loves us unconditionally, yet we keep adding conditions. "Okay, fine," we say reluctantly, "but once we accept God's grace, we'd better get our act together. We had better be successful or we won't be worthy of His grace." We just cannot believe God can grace even our "failures."

The Northern California State Finals in high school track and field were hosted in our town a few years ago. Each participant had won at least one event in the regional competition in order to be eligible for this meet. During the warmups for the girls' 3200-meter run (eight laps around the track), I noticed one girl who appeared to be limping badly. When I looked closer, I saw that her legs seemed to be twisted and her feet were turned in at an awkward angle. I couldn't believe she was actually in the race and assumed she was a manager who, when the race began, would be given all the warmup jerseys to keep until it was over. The bell rang indicating it was time for the contestants to line up. She was not a manager; she stood with the rest of the girls.

When the gun went off she began racing. I assumed that although she was limping, she would be able to keep up with the rest of the runners. I was wrong. After the first lap she was a quarter of a lap behind, and by the time everyone else had finished, she still had one lap to go all by herself. As she went down the backstretch, I could see the agony in her face. Every step she took was excruciatingly painful, but she would not stop. Without realizing it, all of us in the stands had risen to our feet. We were all cheering her on. As she passed by the front of the stands, the noise was overpowering. We were all screaming in unison, "Go! Go! Go!" When she finally crossed the finish line, the crowd erupted in a lengthy ovation. The race was a very long time ago. To this day I have no idea who won the girls' 3200, *but I will never forget the girl who was last.* (By the way, I discovered how she ended up in the race. She was from a small-school region and was the only person to run in the 3200. Most girls with her disability would have declined to run in a state final, but, thank God, she didn't.)

The grace of God says to you and to me, "I can make last place more significant than first place. I will use prostitutes to teach others about gratitude. I will use lepers as examples of cleanliness. I will take men who persecute the church and make them its pillars. I will take the dead and give them life. I will take uneducated fishermen and make them fishers of men." God's grace does not exist to make us successful. God's grace exists to point people to a love like no other love they have ever known. A love outside the lines.

GRACE INCLUDES THE EXCLUDED

The voices start again, "Yeah, right, I'm glad God loves outside the lines, because that is where I was, but how does this grace thing work? I mean, I can believe this stuff, but then what?" When you are loved outside the lines, you start living outside the lines. Let me give you a couple of examples:

> Our town is very small by California standards—one traffic light and six thousand residents. One Sunday morning I was preaching about the unconditional love of God, a love that was outside the lines and resulted in the church loving outside the lines. Our church is different from most; the congregation (probably thanks to Maria—see chapter 2) feels free to interrupt me during my sermons. Just as I was finishing, a sixteen-year-old girl said, "This is a good sermon, Pastor, but I was thinking that if we are supposed to love outside the lines, then I know how we can do it. In three weeks the

Siskiyou County Fair is coming, and with the fair come the 'carnies.'" (The "carnies" are itinerant workers who operate the rides of the traveling carnival. Every year the carnies are the talk of our rural town. Most of them are tough-looking and scary with lots of tattoos, huge muscles, and hard-looking faces. People always make derogatory comments about them.)

The high school girl continued, "I was thinking that instead of making fun of the carnies, maybe we should have a dinner and welcome them to town."

The church agreed, and this young girl organized the entire event. She called the manager of the fair for permission, called the owner of the carnival to see if they would want a dinner. The carnival owner suggested a lunch just before the fair opened. "Okay," said the girl, "we will barbecue hamburgers and cheese-burgers and have salads, desserts, and soft drinks. All you can eat. How many can we expect?" After some thought, the owner said to expect fifty.

The day of the lunch about twenty people from the church showed up to help serve. There was enough food for seventy. At twelve-thirty when the lunch was to begin, only four carnies showed up. By one-thirty, however, we hadn't served 50 carnies, or 75 carnies, or even 150 carnies. We had served *200* carnies. When it looked like we would run out of food, the young girl came running up to me, the pastor, and said, *"We're running out of food. GET SOME!"* We did.

When the lunch was over, numerous carnies came up to the young girl and thanked her. One older lady who had been working carnivals for a long time said, "I have been doing carnivals for forty years, and this is the first time I've been welcomed to town." The all-you-can-eat carnie lunch has been going for seven years now, all because a teenage girl was naive enough to believe God loved a group of carnies as much as He loved her.

Naive grace is the kind of love that wants everyone to be included instead of finding ways to exclude. Jesus Christ was naive enough to love anyone and everyone. Even adulterers. A woman was caught in the act of adultery. The Pharisees and religious leaders dragged her to Jesus, humiliating her in front of the crowds. The woman was a pawn in the hands of those who would discredit Jesus. They cared nothing about her; what they cared about was maintaining their hold over the people.

"Okay, Jesus," they said arrogantly, "what should we do with this woman? Moses and the Law say stone her. What do You say?"

Jesus was not ambiguous about sin and certainly did not condone adultery, and luckily He wasn't ambiguous about grace. Jesus said one sentence. A few words. "If any one of you is without sin, let him be the first to throw a stone at her." Her accusers dropped off one by one.

Why didn't *Jesus* admonish her? Why didn't He point out where her lifestyle would cause her to end up? Why didn't He remind her of the Scriptures she was violating? This woman knew all about condemnation. She knew the Scriptures, knew the sad and empty consequences of her lifestyle, *but she didn't know about grace*. Jesus introduced her to a scandalous grace and then reminded her, "Leave your life of sin."

I love this story and decided to put myself in it as a member of the crowd in the temple, just an ordinary observer.

I left the crowd early. I didn't think I could stomach a stoning. I had seen too many in my lifetime, but I was intrigued with this Jesus person. I circled around to watch as one by one each person left the woman until she was standing alone. I will never forget the look on her face—distant, blank, no defiance left in her. It was obvious she had given up. Her shoulders were slumped forward, her face looked old, deep lines of pain etched upon it. She was not humiliated by this experience; she was beyond humiliation. She was no stranger to the disdain of men. She had suffered abuse before—most of her life, really. Suffering abuse was her companion, her place.

I watched her standing there for what seemed like hours. The silence was deafening—you could actually hear the footsteps of those leaving. She just stood there with Jesus. He had knelt down while all of this was happening, writing in the sand. She looked straight ahead, ignoring Him, ignoring all of us, but when everyone had left I could see her look ever so slightly first to the left and then the right. When she realized she was alone, I could see the amazed look on her face. She couldn't believe it! All of her accusers were gone! I swear to you, it looked as if the wrinkles on her face suddenly disappeared. Her eyes, no longer dull and colorless, seemed to flash in the desert sun. She looked at Him for the first time, trying to take Him all in, trying to understand this strange man who acted like no man she had ever met. He said something to her. I couldn't hear what He said, but I did notice the tears. They came slowly at first, then drowned her face in a lifetime of sorrow. She cried a long time, as though her soul were cleansing itself.

I will never forget what Jesus did next. He stood facing her, staring intently at her tear-soaked face. She was standing much straighter, her shoulders upright and strong. He reached down to her and gently, tenderly, wiped the tears from her face. She stopped crying. He cupped her face in His hands and bent down and kissed her on the forehead. He held her face a very long time, not really looking at her but through her, as though He were looking at her heart, at all the scars on her soul. It was as if He was healing her soul, looking her sin away. And then, abruptly, He let go of her face, turned to leave, turned back, and . . . *winked*.

The grace of God is indiscriminate, foolish, impractical, unrealistic, crazy, and naive. If God is not careful, people like you and me might actually believe Jesus Christ is winking at us . . . just like a little child.

CHAPTER NINE

Childlike Faith

*"Let the little children come to me, and do not hinder them,
for the kingdom of God belongs to such as these. I tell you
the truth, anyone who will not receive the kingdom of God
like a little child will never enter it."*[1]

*"From the lips of children and infants
you have ordained praise."*[2]

I DON'T KNOW HOW OLD I WAS, BUT I REMEMBER WRITING A LONG note to Santa and leaving him cookies and milk one Christmas Eve. I hated Christmas Eve. It was the longest night of the year, a deliberate plot on the part of all adults to delay Christmas. I went to bed early, only to awaken every few minutes, listening for Santa, wondering if I should sneak into the living room to see if the jolly old man had deposited my presents yet.

When the first rays of light broke into my bedroom, I awoke to mysterious noises coming from the direction of our living room. Sitting up in my bed, I tried to decipher what I was hearing. Whatever the sounds, I knew I had heard them before. And then I knew. I leaped out of bed and ran into the living room. *It was a train! An electric train!*

My mom and dad were there waiting to see the look of surprise on my face. They were not disappointed. For a moment I stood there frozen, my eyes stretching to take it all in, my face charged with electricity, the words escaping from my lips before I could think, *"A train! A TRAIN!"* I ran over to the console where my father was sitting and started to grab the speed control.

My mom and dad both spoke up: "Wait!" Confused, I stopped. My mom and dad went on to explain that electric trains were fragile, and you had to be very, very careful when operating them.

I soon found how complicated electric trains were. Every time I ran the controls my parents seemed nervous and worried, and would interrupt my engineering attempts with the usual cautions: "Slow down!" "Oops, watch out for the turn!" "Careful!"

Later in the day we were visited by family and neighbors,

and the electric train became the hit of the adults. All the men crowded around the controls and were having the time of their lives playing with my train. I tried to squeeze into the crowd of men so I could play with my train, but no one seemed to notice. What did a four-year-old do when his dad and all his relatives hogged his electric train? I did what I had to do.

I called the police. I very determinedly walked over to the phone, picked it up, and asked the operator to connect me with a policeman so I could report a hijacked electric train. When my dad was alerted to what I was doing, he laughed. Then he explained to the operator what was going on and promptly asked everyone to move back so I could operate my electric train.

Perhaps as you worked your way through this book you have thought, *Yeah! I want to rediscover my childlike faith again! I want to find the place of passion, curiosity, wonder, and grace. I'm ready to live life with wild abandon. I'm ready to listen to the thin silence of God and play again.* But already the voices of responsibility and predictability are starting: "Wait!" "Slow Down!" "Careful!" Already the dull-shaped words are racing to the front of your mind: *impractical, frivolous, irresponsible, counterproductive,* and *idealistic.* They are trying to rob you of the life you have been longing to live, the joy you've been waiting to experience. Jesus is standing at the other side of those words. He is moving the critics and the saboteurs away and telling you, "Go for it!"

This has been a very impractical call to revert to your childhood. Going back there will not be easy, but I would like to give you some encouragement as you face the dream stealers head-on.

Pray Like a Child

Praying was easy when we were children. No embarrassment, no formulas, no clichés and religiously correct God words; we just prayed whatever words came to our minds. One of my favorite children's prayers is:

Dear Jesus,
I want to thank you for going up there on the Cross for us every Good Fridays.
    You must be real happy when the weekend is over.
Thanks,
Anita (age 11)[3]

Children tell God what they are genuinely thinking. They are honest, simple, and direct. They understand that God is listening, and they understand that prayers are very important. Somehow when we become adults, we forget how important praying is. So if you and I are going to be like little children, we must not forget our prayers.

Billy Graham came to Sacramento, the capital of California, two years ago to hold his crusade at the Arco Arena, just north of downtown. The night before the crusade was to begin, choir rehearsal went late. One of the members of the choir was driving home through downtown when he noticed a man slumped over on the steps of the capitol building. It was cold outside, almost midnight, and not the safest of places to be. The choir member decided he could not ignore the plight of this poor, homeless man. He was nervous as he approached the man, not knowing what to expect. The homeless man was crouched almost cocoonlike on the steps, and the choir member reached out and gently touched his shoulder. "Sir, can I help you?" he said. "Are you okay?" The man looked up. It was Billy Graham. He was praying for the city of Sacramento.[4]

Billy Graham is famous. He has people all over the world praying for him and his crusades, but he still knows where the power of his crusades comes from: his moments praying with his Savior. In this day of TV evangelists with their flashy clothes, sophisticated fund-raising, limos, gold necklaces, and Learjets, it's nice to know that one evangelist still trusts the silent, unflashy power of prayer. Billy Graham has not forgotten to say his prayers. And neither should we.

Don't Be Limited by Adult Vocabulary

Little children don't have a large vocabulary . . . *of words*, but their vocabulary outside of words is massive. It's not limited to but includes hugs, winks, tears, squeezes, laughter, screaming, jumping, hopping, skipping, dancing, and silence. When you and I decide to be childlike, let's remember the vocabulary of children.

An elderly friend of mine went to the hospital to be with one of his children who was dying of cancer. During those last few days with his son, my friend was continually interrupted by well-meaning Christian friends who came by to offer advice, help, prayers, tapes, books, and encouragement. Even though he knew everyone was trying to be helpful, the old man could hardly wait for the people to leave. Then one evening, late, a fifty-year-old construction worker walked into the room. His son had been killed in a tragic car accident the year before. He slid a chair next to my friend, reached out, grabbed his hand, and said nothing. My friend told me he never wanted this man to leave. His silence was healing, strengthening, encouraging, understanding, and . . . enough! The construction worker understood the language of children. He knew what his friend needed: no words.

Yes, our childhood vocabulary grows as we grow, and as we learn more words, we forget the nonverbal vocabulary of our childhood. But even when we're older, our hearts sometimes remember.

It was our eldest boy's wedding, and he asked his younger brother to be best man. One of the roles of the best man is to give a toast to the new groom at the wedding reception, and Trent had taken a great deal of time to craft a toast that would honor their friendship and their love for each other. At the reception, when his time came, Trent stepped up to the microphone to begin his tribute to his brother.

The tribute never happened; that is, the *verbal* tribute.

Each time Trent would try to say his prepared words, they would stick in his throat and he would be overwhelmed by emotion. There was a long period of silence accompanied by the constant flowing of tears from Trent's eyes. Finally, after many frustrated attempts, Trent raised his glass and said, "To my brother!"

Trent was disappointed he was not able to speak the words he so desperately wanted to say.

I have thought about the evening many times, and my conclusion has always been the same. Trent said more about his love and admiration for his brother in his *silence* and his tears than he ever could have with his words. His silence was a loud expression of his love for his brother; the childlike shedding of tears was more profound than thousands of words.

Do not be afraid to use your childlike vocabulary in place of your adult vocabulary.

Ask for Help!

Children are not afraid to ask for help. They have no problem admitting they are in over their heads. To children, a call for help is a proud expression of their dependency on those who love them. Adults, on the other hand, are anxious about calling for help. We are hesitant to admit we're in trouble. Calling for help is humiliating; it's an admission of need, an acknowledgment of weakness, and we don't want to experience that kind of humiliation.

A young, determined woman who is also a close friend of mine spent a week in Hawaii with her husband to celebrate their tenth wedding anniversary. Ever since I have known her, she has possessed a fierce independence which has contributed to her quick success in the business community. Throughout her life she has overcome numerous obstacles on her own, without anyone's help or advice.

One afternoon as she and her husband lay out on the beach seeking a politically incorrect tan, the wet, sticky heat of the Hawaiian summer caused her to jump into the ocean to cool off. She had been snorkeling most of the day and decided to take her mask, but because she was just going in for a cool-down, she left her fins on the shore. Fascinated by the fish, she decided to casually look around while she cooled off. Surprised by a school of rare, colorful fish, she lost herself in playful pursuit, thinking more about the fish than about how far she was drifting from shore. When she finally looked up, it was clear she had unknowingly been caught in a riptide. She was amazed how far away the beach was. Quickly realizing her dilemma, she swam hard for shore.

It didn't take her long to realize she was in trouble. Every stroke she made left her farther from shore, rather than closer to it, which caused her to swim even harder. She was not making headway but was losing ground. Because of her determination, she increased her strokes. She would not give up; she would not be defeated by the current; the force of her will would overcome the riptide. But currents and riptides are not easily convinced. As her strength began to give out, she realized finally that she was in grave danger of drowning. Drowning happened to other people, not to her. She had never before experienced complete and total exhaustion, the kind that causes the body to stop functioning.

In desperation, she frantically began waving her arms and screaming for help. Even yelling was difficult. Luckily, as she was perilously close to giving in to drowning, a lifeguard heard her weakening screams and made it to her just in time. She lost control of her bowel movements, and when dragged onto the shore could not move. It took almost an hour before she gained enough strength to sit up. As she relayed the story to me, she said sheepishly, "Mike, do you know how hard it is to ask for help?"

It *is* hard to ask for help. Childlike faith is not for people who need a little help; it is for people who are desperate, who are at the end of their rope. Faith is for those who are not too proud to wave their arms and admit they are drowning.

Faith is not religious positive thinking. It's not a motivational course, a pep talk, an exercise in positive self-imaging. Faith is for the helpless. It is a humiliation, out of which humility is birthed. We do not come to faith to find the extra punch we need to make it over the hill. We come to faith because we are exhausted, weakened, ready to give up. Faith is more than giving up, it is giving in.

If we want to experience a childlike faith, we must be more than willing to admit our helplessness.

Embrace Your Ordinariness

Children find the ordinary as intriguing as the extraordinary. They can be as easily captivated by a bug on the window as they can be by the launch of the *Discovery*. What is extraordinary to a child this minute will be ordinary the next. In other words, children have an innate leveling mechanism that keeps reality in perspective. They are neither overly impressed with power or unimpressed with the ordinary. Faith allows us to recognize the indiscriminate power of God that takes the ordinary and makes it *extra*ordinary.

A year ago I traveled to Canada for a youth event. I was only there for three days. As usual, I had crammed into my three days more than I could possibly accomplish. I spoke three times, visited some classes, had dinner with a young couple new to youth ministry, spent an afternoon sightseeing in the mountains north of Vancouver . . . and visited a monastery.

Vespers were at five in the afternoon, and because I was late I drove like a maniac into the mountains where the cathedral was located, arriving after they had already begun. Twenty or so monks were participating, and I was ready to experience the presence of God. My cluttered lifestyle had me desperately in need of that presence. I longed for the living water of silence and worship. I felt claustrophobic with my busyness and needed to feel the breath of God on my soul. Maybe this one-hour experience could reconnect me with the living water of God.

I was very disappointed.

Instead of being led in worship by quiet, centered, godly men who by their simple attire and presence would bring me to the feet of God, I was met by twenty obviously bored, distracted, sleepy, strange, grumpy old monks. The younger ones in the group tried, but even they seemed impatient with the routine and were anxious to leave. These men were not spiritual and godly, they were human and flawed and were obviously having a "bad God day."

It wasn't until a year later that I began to understand the gift those monks gave me. What I had wanted from them was a dose of religion; what I received was a dose of reality. I wanted to experience the "otherness" of sainthood, but what I was given was the presence of genuine saints. Genuine saints are genuine human beings who are capable of boredom and bad God days. Grumpiness, idiosyncrasies, pouting, and pettiness are all present in saints as well as the rest of us. Silence and solitude are not instant cures to busyness. They are lifetime commitments worked out in the real world of schedules and flawed human beings. Monks may not have to deal with television and cluttered schedules, but they have to deal with other monks. They have to deal with boredom, frustration, self-image, meaning, and loneliness. In other words, they have to deal with the same issues we all have to deal with. These "ordinary" saints encouraged me.

Childlike faith is for ordinary people. People like you and me who know our flaws only too well. We are familiar with our inconsistencies and our unsaintliness and understand the good news of the gospel—Jesus Christ liberates us from the oppression of our ordinariness and gives us permission to trust God to make us extraordinary.

Don't Stop Playing

There is a great story making the rounds about a well-known pianist, Ignace Jan Paderewski. His concert in New York had been sold out for six months. On the night of the concert those who came were dressed in tuxedos and fancy dresses. A mother brought her nine-year-old son because he was beginning to complain about his piano lessons, and she thought hearing a great pianist might motivate him to keep practicing.

You can dress a nine-year-old in a tuxedo, but he's still nine. Restless and impatient, he continually had to go to the bathroom and, much to the irritation of those sitting by them, kept walking back and forth. Finally the mother became exasperated, grabbed her son by the shoulders, and sat him down hard in his seat. "Now stay there and don't move!" she said sternly. But a few minutes later, while the mother was distracted by the person on the other side of her, the boy slipped out to the aisle. The mother turned to see her son walking toward the stage, where a huge Steinway piano was standing. Panicky, she yelled at him to come back. Startled, the little boy panicked, ran toward the stage, ran up the stairs straight to the piano, sat down, and began to play "Chopsticks." People in the audience were furious.

"Get that kid off the stage!"

"This is an outrage!"

"What is this boy doing here!"

As the startled ushers began moving toward the young boy, Paderewski heard the commotion and looked out of his dressing room. He saw the boy playing "Chopsticks." He quickly grabbed his tuxedo jacket, walked to the edge of the backstage area, and then stepped into full view of the audience. There was a collective hush. Everyone wondered what the great pianist would do. The boy, oblivious to what was happening, continued to play. Paderewski came up behind him, went down on his knees, and whispered in the little boy's ear, "Don't stop. Keep on playing. You're doing great." While the boy continued to play, the great pianist put his arms around the boy and began playing a concerto based on the tune of "Chopsticks." While the two played, Paderewski kept saying to the boy, "Don't stop. Keep on playing."

As you look at your life, as you contemplate embracing the faith of a little child, as you wonder what difference your bumbling, flawed life will make, I hope you have heard in the pages of this book God's whispering voice, "Don't stop. Keep on playing. You're doing great."

One day we shall all be gathered in that great concert hall of God, and we will hear the glorious beauty of the concerto God was playing while you and I plunked out our childlike version of "Chopsticks."

Notes

Introduction

1. *The Interpreter's Bible*, vol. 8, ed. George Buttrick (Nashville: Abingdon, 1952), p. 265.

Chapter One

1. A. W. Tozer, *The Knowledge of the Holy* (New York: Harper & Row, 1961), p. 26.
2. Douglas Copeland, *Life After God* (New York: Pocket Books, 1995), p. 51.
3. Alan Jones, *Passion for Pilgrimage* (San Francisco: HarperSanFrancisco, 1995), p. 146.
4. Robert Farrar Capon, *The Astonished Heart* (Grand Rapids: Eerdmans, 1996), p. 120.
5. What I mean by "ruins" is a holy disruption where Jesus turns my life upside-down in order to make it right-side up.
6. Tozer, p. 26.
7. Jack Canfield and Mark Victor Hansen, *Chicken Soup for the Soul* (Deerfield Beach, Fla.: Health Communications, 1993), pp. 207-208.
8. Frederick Buechner, *The Hungering Dark* (New York: Seabury Press, 1969), p. 29.
9. Juan Carlos Ortiz paraphrases Matthew 6:33 to reflect modern culture's standard of living. "Seek ye first what you are going to eat, what you are going to wear, which house you are going to buy, which car you are going to drive, which job you are going to take, who you are going to marry—and then, if any time is left, and if it's not too uncomfortable, please do something for the kingdom of God." Ortiz, *Disciple* (Carol Stream, Ill.: Creation House, 1975), p. 23.
10. C. S. Lewis, *The Lion, the Witch, and the Wardrobe* (New York: Collier Books, 1950), pp. 160-161.

Chapter Two

1. Abraham Heschel, *Man's Quest for God* (New York: Scribner's & Sons, 1954), p. 139.

2. Hans Küng, as quoted in Bob Bensen and Michael W. Benson, *Disciplines for the Inner Life* (Waco, Tex.: Word, 1985), p. 133.

3. Dan Taylor, *The Myth of Certainty* (Dallas: Word, 1986), pp. 123-124.

4. As quoted in *Harvard Diary* by Robert Coles, (Crossroad, NY: NY, 1988) p. 14.

5. I have many questions for God as well. Why did my little daughter get cancer at eighteen months old? Why would You choose me to be Your church when You know me so well? Why, when everything is going well, can I hear Your voice and see Your tracks, but the moment something goes wrong You are nowhere to be found?

6. Life-giving questions like: What is my calling? Where do I find meaning? Where does forgiveness come from? How do I serve others? How can I learn how to love my enemies?

7. Alan Jones, *Passion for Pilgrimage* (San Francisco: HarperSanFrancisco, 1995), p. 84.

8. I can think of many questions we need to guard. What is God like? Why is there evil? What does love mean? What is justice? What is the nature of forgiveness? And on and on.

9. Henri Nouwen, *In the Name of Jesus* (New York: Paulist Press, 1966), p. 10.

Chapter Three

1. Dan Taylor, *The Myth of Certainty* (Dallas: Word, 1986), p. 124.

2. Juan Carlos Ortiz, *Cry of the Human Heart* (Carol Stream, Ill.: Creation House, 1977), p. 101.

3. For more on this amazing story, read Sarah Dey Carvalho, *The Street Kids of Brazil* (Hodder & Stoughton Ltd, 1996).

4. Bill Harley, told on NPR's *All Things Considered*, July 11, 1995.

Chapter Four

1. Anonymous author, quoted in James Cox, ed., *Best Sermons*, from a sermon by Rabbi Edward Paul Cohn (San Francisco: Harper & Row, 1988), p. 376.

2. George Bernanos, *The Diary of a Country Priest* (New York: Carroll and Graf, 1935), p. 235.

3. Eugene Peterson, *Living the Message* (San Francisco: HarperSanFrancisco, 1996), p. 13.

Chapter Five

1. Robert Bensen, *Between the Dreaming and the Coming True* (San Francisco: HarperSanFrancisco, 1997), p. 55.

2. John Claypool, *Stories Jesus Still Tells* (New York: McCracken Press, 1993), p. 16.

3. Warner, unpublished. ©1996.
4. Adapted from Robert Fulghum, *All I Really Need to Know I Learned in Kindergarten* (New York: Villard Books, 1989), pp. 83-85.
5. Eugene Peterson, *Working the Angles* (Grand Rapids: Eerdmans, 1987), p. 10.
6. Sue Monk Kidd, *When the Heart Waits* (San Francisco: HarperSanFrancisco, 1990), p. 22.
7. Kidd, p. 28.
8. C. S. Lewis, *The Horse and His Boy* (New York: Collier Books, 1954), pp. 155-159.

Chapter Six
1. Sue Monk Kidd, *When the Heart Waits* (San Francisco: HarperSanFrancisco, 1990), p. 71.
2. Saint Augustine, as quoted in Alan Jones, *Passion for Pilgrimage* (San Francisco: HarperSanFrancisco, 1995), p. 35.
3. Will Willimon, *Leadership Journal*, summer 1994.
4. Matthew 13:45-46.
5. Based on a story told to me by Dr. Chapman Clark, chair of the Youth Ministry department, Fuller Theological Seminary.

Chapter Seven
1. John Claypool, *Stories Jesus Still Tells* (New York: McCracken Press, 1993), p. 162.
2. Abraham Heschel *Man Is Not Alone: A Philosophy of Religion* (New York: Noonday, 1951), p. 78.
3. C. S. Lewis, *The Voyage of the Dawn Treader* (New York: Collier Books, 1952), pp. 159-160.
4. Barbara Taylor, "Preaching the Terrors," *Leadership* 13 (spring 1992), pp. 42-45.

Chapter Eight
1. Stuart Hample and Eric Marshall, *Children's Letters to God* (New York: Workman Publishing, 1991).
2. Brennan Manning, *The Signature of Jesus* (Old Tappan, N.J.: Chosen Books, 1988), pp. 125-126.

Chapter Nine
1. Luke 18:16-17.
2. Matthew 21:16.
3. David Heller, *Dear God: Children's Letters to God* (New York: Perigee Books, 1994), p. 118.
4. Told to me by Pastor Ray Johnston.

Author

MIKE YACONELLI has been working with young people for almost forty years. He is the owner of Youth Specialties, an international organization that trains and provides resources for over 100,000 youth workers worldwide. Youth Specialties was cofounded by Mike Yaconelli and Wayne Rice in 1968.

Mike lives in Yreka, California, a rural northern California town where he is lay pastor of Grace Community Church, a small church "for those who don't like church." He and his wife, Karla, are now discovering what it is like to adjust to a cavernous house where their five children used to live. Mark (thirty-one), Trent (twenty-eight), Lisa (twenty-five), Jill (twenty-three), and Jessica (nineteen) are now either going to college, working, dancing, parenting, playing guitar, or all of the above.

Mike (fifty-five) is a local high school board member and the proud grandfather of two-year-old Noah and newborn Joseph, sons of Mark and Jill. He breezed through his four-year college education in ten years and finally graduated from San Diego State University with a degree in communications. Oh . . . Mike speaks a lot too!

BOOKS TO HELP YOU SATISFY YOUR CURIOSITY ABOUT GOD'S WORK IN YOUR LIFE

Righteous Sinners

Righteous Sinners examines faith, grace, and works and the conflicting teaching that abounds on this issue to help you come to a clearer understanding of what it means to be a "righteous sinner."

Righteous Sinners
(Ron Julian) $12

The River Within

Do you feel burned out or bored when it comes to your Christian walk? *The River Within* will help you regain the passion and excitement of following God.

The River Within
(Jeff Imbach) $15

Experiencing God's Forgiveness

This book will help you examine the depth of your sin and guilt in order to appreciate the amazing extent of God's forgiveness in your life.

Experiencing God's Forgiveness
(John Ensor) $12

Get your copies today at your local bookstore, or call (800) 366-7788 and ask for offer **#2034**.

NAVPRESS ◖●◗

BRINGING TRUTH TO LIFE
www.navpress.org

Prices subject to change without notice.